SIBLING BEREAVEMENT

SIBLING BEREAVEMENT
Helping Children Cope with Loss

Ann Farrant

CASSELL

Cassell
Wellington House
125 Strand
London WC2R 0BB

PO Box 605
Herndon
VA 20172

First published 1998

British Library Cataloguing in-Publication Data
A catalogue record for this book is available from the British Library.

ISBN 0304-70204-8 (hardback)
     0304-70205-6 (paperback)

Typeset by Textype Typesetters, Cambridge
Printed and bound in Great Britain by Redwood Books, Trowbridge, Wiltshire

CONTENTS

In memory of Rosamund Sarah Farrant
(31 August 1962 to 23 January 1966)

INTRODUCTION
Background to the book

Writing this book has been a very personal journey. It was prompted by experiences in my own family following the sudden death of my first-born child, a daughter called Rosamund, aged three years and five months. At the time of her death my second daughter was only fourteen months old and I was seven months pregnant with my third child, another daughter. The anguish of Rosamund's loss was intense. Relatives and friends did their best to comfort me, but I felt hammered into the ground by the weight of the grief. However, there was still my surviving daughter to care for and the imminent arrival of another child to take into account. Somehow I found the strength to carry on living, albeit in a state of great distress.

If I had known then what I know now, perhaps I would have tried to manage things differently. But shock and grief alter one's normal perceptions and the best that most people can do during traumas of this kind is to muddle through. A bereaved parent finds it difficult to function at all, let alone take in what is going on for other people. Lucy, my remaining daughter, appeared to be all right as far as I could tell. The new baby, Charlotte, arrived safely and life began to assume some sort of normality – whatever that means in the context of the aftermath of bereavement.

I had read somewhere of the shock experienced by children on discovering, by chance, that there had been another child in the family, a child who had died. So I made a point of talking to my four daughters – Lucy and Charlotte were followed by Emma and Katy – about their older sister Rosamund. All this came later when, as I perceived it, they were old enough to understand. What I did not realize was that Lucy had not been given space in which to come to terms with her own bereavement at the time that it happened. The prevailing wisdom at that time, the late 1960s, was that small children were unlikely to be affected by major events such as death. I believe I thought this to be true. Or perhaps I just wanted it to be.

In my own defence, I have to say that I did not know how to begin to explain Rosamund's sudden disappearance. Lucy didn't ask; how could she? At a pre-verbal stage, it is not easy for a young child to communicate the complex thoughts and fears stirred up by being in a household plunged in gloom. I can't remember if I attempted to offer any kind of explanation even on a simple level. I rather think I said nothing and tried to appear 'normal'. But of course I was nothing of the kind. I had changed. Her father had changed. The whole family set-up had changed.

The crunch came when Lucy was fifteen. She had been admitted to hospital for the removal of an inflamed appendix and was put in an adult ward where there were some quite unpleasant cases. During Lucy's stay there – longer than expected because she developed complications – there was news of another death in the family, that of a second cousin of whom she was particularly fond, and her grandfather was taken into intensive care following a heart attack. It was a worrying time, but, even so, Lucy appeared unduly anxious, both about her own health and about what was going on for everybody else.

Soon after her return from hospital we spent a family holiday in Scotland. It was a very welcome break for us all, but Lucy still seemed very fragile emotionally. It was during this fortnight away from home that she started to communicate in a 'baby' voice. Not all the time, but every now and then, she would hold a conversation in which she assumed 'baby talk'. It was mildly amusing at first, but irritating too. Certainly, at that stage, I didn't attach any particular significance to it.

Matters came to a head one Sunday lunchtime. Lucy failed to respond to a call to join the family at lunch and when I went up to her bedroom she launched into her 'baby' talk. I lost my temper. She burst into tears. The crying was out of all proportion to my having snapped at her. She was weeping as if overwhelmed by some deep grief, the sort of anguished wailing I had succumbed to after Rosamund died. Instinctively and suddenly, I knew there must be a connection.

As soon as lunch was over and the others had been persuaded to go out for the afternoon I settled down with Lucy. I wasn't at all sure what to do, but just followed my instinct to ease her pain. She seemed so vulnerable, so defenceless and small. I held her close and started by asking her to put on her 'baby' voice. Then I asked her what was the matter. I said I was there for her, that I cared, that I knew she was in sorrow. I went on holding her and making soothing noises, very much in the way that I would try to comfort a crying baby.

It took some time before Lucy began to speak. When she did, she had somehow moved herself back in time to the period following her sister's death. It was a remarkable and harrowing experience. Lucy became deeply distressed. She clung to me as if her life depended on it and poured out a torrent of grief and woe which seemed unending. All the while I went on holding her and reassuring her of my support. In effect, she was reliving the sheer horror of the sudden loss of the much-loved older sister who had cuddled and loved her, played silly games, made her laugh, been her first friend. Out too came enormous anxiety about what had happened, fear that somehow it might have been her fault, fear that she too would disappear, fear that Mummy and Daddy might suddenly go away. It was heartbreaking stuff, but strangely reassuring too, for I had often worried about Lucy's volatile emotional state and her dramatic reactions to minor upsets, without ever really understanding that she was suffering somewhere deep inside from the effect of losing her big sister. So many unanswered questions were suddenly made clear. So much catching up could now be done. At last there was a chance for Lucy to go through the process of mourning which had been denied her.

It was a daunting prospect and one which I knew needed expert help. Lucy started counselling sessions with a psychotherapist, an excellent woman, who was able to guide her through the complex business of coming to terms with the bereavement and its aftermath. It was a long and painful process, but very healing too. Lucy and I also had a great deal of work to do, putting together the missing pieces, sharing our grief. It wasn't always easy, for I had moved on from that terrible time and it was distressing to stir it up again. Painful, too, to realize how unknowing I had been of my little daughter's grief at the time of her sister's death. If only we could have mourned together at the outset. If only I had been able to find some way of understanding her fears and reassuring her. I still don't know how this could have been achieved, given the very young age she was at the time and with so few verbal skills.

During this time I thought, too, about the death of my older brother and its impact on my life. The significant difference, comparing my experience with Lucy's, was that I was an adult when the death occurred. My brother and I were both in our twenties at the time and neither of us had been living at home with our parents for several years. The old family was already dispersed. I was part of a new family, with husband and young children, and, although I sought to comfort my stricken parents, I was not part of their day-to-day struggle to work through the bereavement. More importantly, as an adult, I was able to make choices about how I dealt with my own loss.

In our discussions Lucy and I often wondered how it must be for other children bereaved of siblings. Was their age a significant factor? Were they given space in which to grieve? How had the death affected them, both at the time it happened and in the years following? We felt it would be helpful to hear some other case histories. This book has arisen out of those discussions.

It has not been my intention to lay down any formulas about how bereaved parents should behave towards their surviving children. There is no 'right' way. Each family, each death, each survivor, is different. Rather, I have let the victims of sibling bereavement tell their own stories and share their conclusions about the experience, in the hope that what they have to say may provide some insight into this emotional minefield.

I am very grateful to all those people who agreed to be interviewed about their often very painful memories of sibling loss and its aftermath. It was a rewarding and enriching experience to hear their stories firsthand, and I have been greatly encouraged by their interest in and support for the project. Some interviewees asked to remain anonymous; their names have been changed. In particular I should like to thank Betty Rathbone, BA, MA, MPhil, AFBPsS, a consultant clinical psychologist, who answered all my questions about the likely effects of sibling bereavement, and my four daughters, who not only encouraged me to write this book but also contributed to it.

CHAPTER 1
Bereavement counselling

'Bereavement counselling' is a comparatively recent term. We usually read about it in the context of some headline-making tragedy. Most press coverage of the M40 mini-bus accident in November 1993, in which twelve schoolchildren died, carried the information that fellow pupils were being offered this service. In May 1994, many newspaper reports of the death in County Tyrone of a teenage girl who killed herself a few days after a close friend had committed suicide included comments from counsellors who spoke of the trauma of loss, especially for adolescents, and the need for skilled help in coming to terms with it. More recently, the murder of sixteen young children at a Dunblane school focused media attention once more on the topic of counselling bereaved youngsters.

It is good that society is recognizing that the tragic deaths of these young people will have a profound effect on their peer group, who will therefore need some expertise in helping them to deal with the aftermath. But is as much care and attention always given to children who suffer bereavement in a less public way, especially when they lose a sibling?

It has long been recognized that those who suffer the loss of someone close to them need to work through the mourning process. In these days of support groups and counselling services there are numerous sources of help for the bereaved. However, the vast majority appear to be for adults; for example, Cruse Bereavement Care for the widowed, the Compassionate Friends for bereaved parents. But what about bereaved children? More particularly, what about children who lose a sibling? In most cases when a child dies, the parents become the main cause for concern. No matter how inadequate they feel, no matter how daunting the prospect of trying to give comfort, most friends and relatives in such a situation do their best to rally round the stricken mother and father.

There's no denying that the parents need all the help they can get, but so, too, do the remaining siblings, and their needs are very often overlooked. If they are very young, the popular assumption is that they are of an age to be 'untouched by the grief', as one well-meaning friend wrote to me of my fourteen-month-old daughter when her sister died. If they are older they may well be ignored or left to fend for themselves, as the adults around them cope with the shocking aftermath of the death of a child. In some cases they may try to take on the burden of attempting to comfort their parents, putting their own feelings on one side in the process. Or they may retreat from the whole emotionally charged atmosphere, acutely aware of the weight of sorrow, but terrified of saying or doing anything which might provoke even more distress and pain. Who can blame parents, suffering the anguish of losing a child, if their usual concerns for all their children are, albeit temporarily, completely shattered?

With hindsight, bereaved parents have spoken to me of their regrets that they 'mishandled' the situation as far as their surviving children were concerned. They have told me of how alone they felt, how inadequate. They have recalled that, on some level, they knew their offspring needed help too, but they didn't have the emotional resources to deal with it.

Adults who lost a brother or a sister many years ago have wept again as they shared with me the misery of seeing the family ripped apart by the tragedy and their sorrow that their own needs for comfort, information and reassurance were not met. They have described the long-term effects of the loss of a sibling, for the death of a child in a family alters that family's structure for ever. The missing youngster had his or her own role in the family, his or her own place. The gap can never be filled, but some surviving siblings may strive to do just that, carrying with them burdens of guilt, inadequacy and resentment.

When a brother or sister dies, the children left behind are mourning not only the loss of that sibling, but also the loss of the shape of the family. Their own position in the pecking order has changed and many find this something of an affront to their own sense of self. Coming to terms with being in a different place in the family is often extremely difficult.

Many of those bereaved of a brother or sister have managed to work through the grieving process at a later date and have found ways of coming to terms with their loss. Indeed, it would be wrong to suggest that lives are ruined by such experiences. It is never too late to start the mourning process. Betty Rathbone, a consultant clinical psychologist, who is head of a child and family centre dealing with disturbed youngsters, told me she believes that those who have endured loss in childhood and managed to work through it can develop into strong, resilient adults, with an instinctive understanding of others' sorrows and a heightened sensitivity.

The important thing is to recognize the 'unfinished business' and to find some way of dealing with it. Ideally, of course, the business of grieving and working through its aftermath is best done at the time of the loss.

CHAPTER 2
Infant mortality

The Victorians dealt with death very differently. The mourning rituals and symbols of grief were of prime importance: the window-blinds drawn down, the dead laid out in a coffin at home so that friends could 'pay their last respects', the black clothes, the mourning rings and brooches – the latter often containing a lock of the loved one's hair – the cards edged with black. People in the street stopped as a funeral cortège went past. Men doffed their hats as the coffin came into view. Very few of these customs have lasted into the latter part of this century and perhaps we are the poorer for their passing.

A hundred years ago high infant mortality rates were a fact of life and children who did survive were not spared from facing the evidence of their own mortality. It seems that there was little escape from the subject. Even if children were fortunate enough not to lose a sibling, their own reading material made much of the whole business of infant death. Many of these Victorian tales were little more than a vehicle for preaching to the young.

The Religious Tract Society, among others, published a series of didactic works in the form of stories for children, many of which contained full accounts of the death of at least one child. They make mawkish reading for our late-twentieth-century eyes. We can only guess at the impact they had on the readers of the time.

Take one example, *Little Blind May*.[1] (The copy in my collection is inscribed 'Ellen Miles. A New Year Gift. January 1878'.) The story is told in the first person by some unnamed observer, who thus has ample opportunity to pass moral judgements at various stages in the narrative. The heroine, eight-year-old May, is the one surviving child out of five siblings. The family has fallen on hard times and is living in the slums of London. The father has taken to drink and, as the story progresses, we learn that May's blindness is the result of his having struck her in a drunken stupor.

May's best friend is an orphan called Tommy, who is encouraged by her to start going to Sunday School. A street urchin, he makes a rather precarious living as a tumbler and odd-job lad, but still manages to use some of his earnings to buy treats for May. She, of course, is virtue personified, so that when, about half-way through the tale, she learns the truth about her disability, she is able to forgive her guilty father and use the occasion to restore his faith. He becomes a reformed character.

By then May is seriously ill, or 'ripening for heaven fast' as her mother puts it. The shock to his system of giving up alcohol has caused the father's health to fail too, and he dies on his wife's breast, with the words, 'Tell May that I will open the gates of glory to her when she comes.' May's declining days are spelled out in the final chapter. On her deathbed she calls Tommy 'brother' for the first time and implores him to be a son to her widowed mother.

> Said May, raising her feeble voice once more, 'I have nothing to leave to all the poor friends who loved me for so long. Tomorrow, when I am cold, cut off my hair, mother, and give a lock of it to each, that they may have some little thing to tell them May did not die without a last thought of love for her friends.' She sank back on the pillows, the death-sweat standing in large drops on her brow. They heard her murmur very faintly, 'Lord Jesus, I come, I come!' and then she seemed too weak for further utterance. The boy and her mother fell on their knees beside her bed, and with voiceless, tearless prayers watched the young life ebbing away. They never knew when she drew her last breath, so gently did she sink; but about midnight the lids of the sightless eyes fell, and mother and son felt that she was now gazing with a new vision on the face of Him she had loved and worshipped on earth.

I recall as a child of about eight being utterly enthralled by one such book. It was called, I believe, *Little Dot* and it came from my grandmother's house. I spent a whole morning reading about Dot, an impossibly angelic waif who was befriended by an elderly grave-digger. In the closing chapters our young heroine perished and the old man had the heart-breaking task of digging a grave for his little friend! It was intended as a moral lesson: be good and pure like little Dot and you too will be assured of a place in heaven. I don't know if I recognized this at the time, but I was certainly overcome by the tragedy of it all. I wept copiously as I reached the end, whereupon my mother seized the book and threw it in the fire, declaring she didn't want me to be upset by rubbish like that.

I can see her point. These stories, wrapping up the pain and grief of bereavement into a sickly parcel of moral teachings and avoiding any suggestion of anger, shock and guilt on the part of those left behind, offer accounts which bear little resemblance to reality. Although I was distressed I was also rather enjoying the pity of it, casting myself in the role of Dot and imagining myself as a corpse, surrounded by weeping relatives. My mother, however, was part of the backlash which followed the Victorian obsession with death and regarded this wallowing as positively unhealthy.

She was not alone in her views; for, in the wake of the Victorian way of dealing with death came a complete swing of the pendulum. It was helped, of course, by vastly improved infant mortality rates. But, whatever the reason, the subject of death became taboo and the role of children in the mourning process all but disappeared.

For several decades it was considered to be quite unhealthy to involve children in such things. No doubt it was done with the best possible motives: those of protecting the young, sparing them pain and grief. Death gradually moved out of the home – quite literally, for whereas in the nineteenth century many deaths took place at home, as time went on care of the terminally ill became part of the hospital routine. Dead bodies were removed to funeral parlours, the bereaved stopped wearing black for months on end, sometimes even at the funeral itself, and many of the other rituals went out of fashion. It was thought not at all proper for young people to be exposed to death in any way. When a death occurred in a family the young were removed from the scene, while the remaining adults went about the funerary business.

When I was about twelve a girl in my class at school died. A gentle, pretty, well-liked girl, she had been away for some time and we had become accustomed to her absence. Nobody had told us why. None of us knew she was dying of cancer. So when the headmistress came in one morning to tell us that this girl had died, a thrill of horror ran through the classroom. Nothing more was said, nor were questions invited. No attempt was made to comfort us. We just carried on with our lessons. As I remember it, there was an unspoken message that somehow it was 'not quite right' to wish to know more or, indeed, to say anything. Looking back, I find myself wishing we had understood more about dying, that some of us at least might have been encouraged to write to her parents expressing our sorrow, sharing with them our memories of their only daughter. It seems wrong that we barely mentioned her passing, even among ourselves.

There was, too, a sense of unreality about the business of her dying. In a morbid way, I think I somehow equated it with the death of Beth in *Little Women*.[2] She was another of those fictional virtuous maidens, the perfect child compared with her three surviving siblings – foolish Meg, hoydenish Jo and selfish Amy. Beth was Little Dot in another setting – the personification of the adage about the good dying young. The description of her death is a masterpiece of sentimentality.

More recent children's literature has begun to bridge the gap in understanding the realities of death. Perhaps at last we are gaining a more middle ground, somewhere between the Victorians' showy sentimentality about death and much of this century's reticence about the subject, especially in front of children.

A Summer to Die[3] tells of a year in the life of two sisters, Molly and Meg, a year during which the older girl dies and the younger girl has to face up to the loss. By making the relationship between the two girls a mixture of affection and friction – they actually have a row on the night when Molly is taken back to hospital for the last time – the author achieves a sense of realism. Neither the dying Molly nor her troubled younger sister is cast in the saintly mould. With none of the Victorian child's preoccupation with death, Meg is quite oblivious of the fact that Molly's illness is terminal. When she understands at last, the grief is beautifully captured. It happens one evening when Meg, tired of the quiet which pervades the house, turns on the radio and persuades her father to dance with her.

> We stood facing each other at the end, and I said suddenly, 'I wish Molly was here.' My mother made a small noise, and when I looked over at her, she was crying. I looked back at Dad in bewilderment, and there were tears on his face, too, the first time I had ever seen my father cry.
>
> I reached out my arms to him, and we both held out our arms to Mom. She moved into them, and as the music started again, another slow, melancholy song from some past summer I couldn't remember, the three of us danced together. . . . I held my arms tight around the two of them as we moved around in a kind of rhythm that kept us close, in an enclosure made of ourselves that kept the rest of the world away, as we danced and wept at the same time. I knew then what they hadn't wanted to tell me, and they knew that I knew, that Molly wouldn't be coming home again, that Molly was going to die.

For the rest of the narrative, Meg has to deal with some difficult emotions – the fear of losing her sister, anger at the unfairness of it all, anxiety about visiting the dying girl in hospital, distress when the death finally happens. Perhaps the closing chapter, when she begins to come to terms with her loss, is less believable, for Meg appears to work through the mourning process comparatively quickly. For all that, *A Summer to Die* is still a vast improvement on many of the fictional accounts of children dying written in previous generations.

For a more realistic view of the effect of sibling death, however, facts, not fiction, provide us with much more credible – and more genuinely moving – accounts.

NOTES

1. Constance Beverley, *Little Blind May*. The Religious Tract Society.
2. Louisa M. Alcott, *Little Women*. First published 1868–9.
3. Lois Lowry, *A Summer to Die*. Kestrel, 1979.

CHAPTER 3
Sibling substitutes

Two of the most celebrated victims of the death of siblings were in fact writers, and for both the experience influenced much of their work. Let us start with the playwright J.M. Barrie. (I will come to the other one, the novelist Charlotte Brontë, in Chapter 10.)

Barrie was only six years old when David, one of his two older brothers, was killed in a skating accident on the eve of his fourteenth birthday in January 1867. For his mother, Margaret Ogilvy, it was an overwhelming tragedy and she never got over it. At first Barrie was jealous of his mother's yearning for her dead son; later, in a vain attempt to assuage her terrible grief, he determined to make himself as much like the dead brother as possible. He spent hours trying to copy David's cheery way of whistling and even went so far as to dress himself in his brother's clothes in order to stand and whistle, with his legs apart and his hands in the pockets of his knickerbockers, just as David had done. To no avail.

> I stood still until she saw me, and then – how it must have hurt her! 'Listen!' I cried in a glow of triumph, and I stretched my legs wide apart and plunged my hands into the pockets of my knickerbockers, and began to whistle.
>
> She lived twenty-nine years after his death. . . . But I had not made her forget the bit of her that was dead; in those nine-and-twenty years he was not removed one day farther from her. . . . When I became a man . . . he was still a boy of thirteen.[1]

As many have pointed out, this profound experience left a permanent mark on the playwright:

> If Margaret Ogilvy drew a measure of comfort from the notion that David, in dying a boy, would remain a boy for ever, Barrie drew inspiration. It would be another thirty-three years before that inspiration emerged in the shape of Peter Pan, but here was the germ, rooted in his mind and soul from the age of six.[2]

I was reminded of J.M. Barrie's efforts to be like his dead brother when I met June Wilde. During our interview, June, who is sixty-five, told me it was the first time she had ever talked to anyone in any detail about the death of her sister.

It is nearly sixty years since June lost her older sister Beryl, and for the greater part of that time she has been trying to live up to the role of her idealized dead sibling. During those years June grew up, worked at various jobs, got married, had two children and became a grandmother. It was only when she reached her late fifties that June recognized that, when her sister died, she effectively lost her own real self.

'It happened quite suddenly and dramatically', June explained. 'I had a period of depressive illness, which is not surprising, an accumulative thing which really only resolved itself in 1986. Round about that time I read a book called *Women Who Love Too Much*[3] and I absolutely identified with that. Of course this was about me and my marriage, but it was also to do with my own development. I quite suddenly realized that I was no longer emotionally attached to my husband and instead of that being a cause for grief it made me feel quite strong. And it was that same summer I picked up a book called *Power for Living*.[4] It came through the post and was addressed to me, although I'll never know to this day who sent it. I read that and suddenly God became real to me. We'd been brought up in the Church and I'd been confirmed but when I was about twenty my faith suddenly went. It went as dramatically as it's returned. And when this all started to happen I had this sense of another self in here. I really did. Another strong self inside my head. And I know I shall never suffer from depression again. I had years of it, it was dreadful. I was suicidal. I should have had some sort of psychiatric help, but I didn't. I had to get through it alone. Trying to be the person I wasn't had crippled me.'

Like Barrie at the time of his brother's death, June was only six years old when her sister died. Beryl, the first-born, was eight, and the baby of the family, Keith, was five. The family lived in the suburbs of Manchester, where all three children had been born.

As June recalled those early days she remembered Beryl as the favourite. 'Keith and I were a similar build, shortish people. I was a quiet child, who liked to sit and read, but Beryl was tall, dark and extroverted. Very gifted and popular. I think she was what nowadays you would call a leader. She was a favourite grandchild too, a general favourite all round.'

In December 1934, June caught chicken-pox and over the same weekend Beryl became ill with violent headaches. At first it was thought that she, too, was sickening for chicken-pox, but it turned out to be much worse than that. By the following Tuesday Beryl was in hospital, seriously ill with meningitis, and on the Thursday she died. 'I couldn't believe it. My mother and father came back to the house – somebody was sitting in for us – and my mother said "Jesus has taken Beryl". I couldn't quite grasp what had happened. From then on there was this terrible feeling of doom about the house. I can remember asking my mother, "Where is the funeral to be?" and she said to me, "It's none of your business." So Keith and I went to a neighbour's for the day. And that was the funeral over.'

I asked June if anything else was said to her and her brother, if anybody made any attempt to explain or to offer reassurance, or, indeed, if she understood the finality of her sister's departure.

'Yes, I understood that she was never coming back. But at the time I don't think my mother was really capable of saying more. She did tell me more about it, but not at the time. It was later on. And I don't think my father said anything at all. It would have been nice for somebody to have sat down and talked to me about it, told me what had happened. I don't think anybody did. Children were not regarded as people then, were they? A sort of alien race.'

Some of June's main memories of the years following her sister's death are of a household steeped in gloom and a sense that she herself must make no reference to the tragedy. 'I can remember all the letters – of condolence, I suppose – coming. They fell through the letter-box in quite a shoal. And Keith and I saying, "Oh, the postman. Look at all the letters he's brought." But nothing was to be said about them. The death was not to be mentioned. That was the feeling I had. My father was a very autocratic and hard man and quite bad-tempered. He certainly never discussed Beryl's death. Like a lot of fathers in those days he wasn't a companion or friend.

'And my mother was never the same again. She had been a rather light-hearted person, always ready to laugh and she obviously enjoyed life. That suddenly all went. A long, long time seemed to go by before I ever heard her laugh again. I heard relatives say that she had "bad nerves"; that's what it was called in those days. I suppose the poor woman was very depressed. In fact I overheard my father say to somebody that had it not been for me and Keith he thought that Ruby, my mother, would have perhaps committed suicide. I think she might have done. And who could have blamed her? To lose her first-born child at the age of eight.

'But she had to keep going. I remember she used to drop things. She'd be lifting a dish and she'd drop it and that was when somebody would say, "Ruby's nerves are very bad." And of course they were. She had nobody to talk it through with. She wore mourning for a year. As I say, there was always this feeling of gloom about the house. The summer after Beryl died we went on a family holiday, to Llandudno, I think. I've got a photo taken of that holiday by a street photographer and there's my mother still in black. And my father looking as miserable as sin. Even that picture looks dreadful. It was meant to be a holiday.'

Apart from the lack of information, the gloomy atmosphere and the absence of any particular concern for her own feelings about her sister's death, there was another factor which caused June tremendous heartache: the constant image of Beryl as the ideal child. 'As a little girl, I realized that Beryl was still the star and I tried to be her. I tried to replace her. I was always getting told, "Beryl wouldn't have done that. Beryl would do this." All the things that Beryl did. She was a very different type of person. I had a quieter nature. I definitely grew up feeling that there was something very wrong with me because I wasn't Beryl. I had this feeling I was a second choice. I felt inadequate.

'We had quite a few aunts and uncles on each side of the family and even years after her death they were calling me "Beryl" by mistake, especially the men. My paternal grandfather certainly could never remember that I was June. If I was out with my mother and she met an acquaintance she hadn't seen for many years, and they'd turn to me and say "Is this your little girl?" she would say, "Yes, but I had another." And I was brushed aside, "Yes, *but* I had another child." The result of this sort of thing, as you grow up, is that you have a very low self-esteem. I think you give yourself rather low expectations too and think any old thing is good enough for you. Why expect more? It's only now, looking back, I can ask "Whilst I was trying to be Beryl, what happened to June?" '

When I asked her to tell me about that little six-year-old June, her eyes filled with tears. Sometimes, she said, she looked at photos of herself when young and thought 'None of it was her fault.' Then she said that, although it was difficult to know for sure, she believed, until her sister died, that she had felt quite all right about herself and hadn't tried to be anyone else. She believed her own personality had been developing along normal lines.

'I think I tried to replace Beryl to cheer them up. I suppose I was doing it for my mother. I wanted to be Beryl for her, because I knew how Beryl was doted on. But it didn't quite work like that. She started to dote on my brother. I felt I couldn't win. Certainly there was this dreadful sense of loss which went on for years. I had slept with Beryl in the same bed. After she died I had difficulty in sleeping and that sparked off years of insomnia. I used to lie in bed and call for my mother. Sometimes she'd come, sometimes she wouldn't. I couldn't sleep, missing Beryl. I missed her dreadfully. But then I also began to resent her because she was held up as this marvellous example. My parents had various photographs enlarged and put them around the house. Then there was this ritual of going to the grave every Saturday with flowers. Keith and I used to drive with my father to a certain florist and buy the flowers and then we'd go and put them on Beryl's grave. But I got very fed up with it. It went on for years.

'And at the age of ten I was still wearing her clothes. It was a very practical thing to do. You can't expect people to throw away perfectly good clothes, but I wasn't too keen on it at all. I also inherited things like her dolls' pram and her dolls. And Beryl had taught me to knit when I was six. I now do a huge amount of knitting; you could say I'm a compulsive knitter. So there you are. I still have a little legacy from her. And one positive thing that came out of the tragedy was that my brother and I drew very close, possibly closer than most brothers and sisters.'

The newly emerged June told me how much she was enjoying life since she recognized that there was no need for her to go on suppressing her true self. 'It's made me feel I'm a much, much stronger person than I used to be. I had low expectations and anything that was dished out to me I tended to think I deserved it. But not any more. I don't think that now. But those earlier years certainly maimed me emotionally and, although I did well at school, I didn't have any ambition to be anything. I had no real push or drive. And another effect it's definitely had on me is that I get very over-anxious about somebody I'm fond of. If they've gone out or gone away I still feel it now, this sort of sick feeling. It was only a few years ago that I realized that this illogical anxiety is because of my sister who went away and didn't come back. And, of course, my parents were over-protective of Keith and me.'

June's father died when she was eighteen. By then her mother had begun to be more communicative about Beryl's death, but for June it was ill-timed. 'By then I didn't want to ask. I didn't want to know. I'd had so many years of how wonderful Beryl was and her photographs around the house. In the end I didn't really want to think about her at all. If you can dislike a dead person I suppose that's what I felt then. But I've forgiven anything a long time ago. If

I'd been in a similar situation who knows how I would have behaved? It was only after I became a mother myself I could appreciate how dreadful it had been for my mother. It was only then that things fell into place.'

Sadly, there never seemed to be the opportunity for June, as an adult, to talk to her mother properly about the death and its aftermath. 'She was still in Manchester and I had moved to Kent. My daughters were coming up to four and two when she died. Had she lived longer I think I would have tried to talk to her.'

Finally, I asked June: if she could reshape the events following Beryl's death, what would she most like to have changed? 'I would like to have been seen as me, not a substitute for somebody else. I suppose that could only have come from my parents and they didn't understand then what was happening. That was the worst thing that happened, that I couldn't be me.'

NOTES

1. J.M. Barrie, *Margaret Ogilvy*. Hodder & Stoughton, 1896.
2. Andrew Birkin, *J.M. Barrie and the Lost Boys*. Constable & Co., 1979.
3. Robin Norwood, *Women Who Love Too Much*. Arrow Books, 1986.
4. James Buckingham, *Power for Living*. Arthur S. De Moss Foundation, 1985.

CHAPTER 4
Dead sibling fantasies

June Wilde's perception that she was somehow inferior to her dead sister is not at all uncommon. According to Betty Rathbone, the psychologist referred to in the Introduction, it is a matter of 'survivor guilt'. The child who outlives a sibling may well feel, 'If one of us had to die it shouldn't have been him or her, it should have been me.' Some parents may recognize this and help to reduce the guilt by talking about the dead child as a real flesh–and–blood person, a mixture of good and bad like most of us. But grief and despair may well get in the way of rational thought, and for some bereaved parents the sense of loss overshadows everything else.

As June herself admitted, her parents could not have realized how detrimental it was for her to have her dead sister held up as a model of virtue. It may seem obvious to outsiders, especially those who have not endured the anguish of losing a beloved child, that such eulogizing might not be helpful to the survivors. But who would imagine that images of a sibling who died before other children were born, a sibling not even known to them, might also cause problems? Yet, strangely enough, such images can have a powerful impact on those who follow later.

Simon Francis and Barbara Dorf, both of whom were born after the death of a son in their respective families, became victims of the idealized dead sibling fantasy. In Simon's case, the perception that his dead brother was, or could have been, all that his parents might have hoped for in a son was not in response to any stated views from anybody in his family. Quite the reverse, in fact.

Now in his early forties, Simon runs a theatrical agency which he and his partner started from scratch. An artistic and creative man, he feels that perhaps now his parents, certainly his mother, are proud of what he has achieved. But as a child he was dogged by the feeling that he was inferior to the brother who had died at birth several years before he was born. By the time Simon arrived there were two sisters, one in her teens, the other a toddler. The brother had been born between these two girls. 'I don't know why, but I felt this brother was a paragon. I had this deep-centred sense of inferiority and I felt a need to prove to my parents that I could be as good as this other child might have been.'

Looking back, Simon believes that one of the reasons for his distorted view of his dead brother was that no one in the family ever talked openly about him. 'In fact, I've never been told officially of his existence. No, I was never told. And I can't remember ever discussing it, even to this day, with my mother. My awareness about having had a brother, who never was, only came about through mutterings and statements which were not directed at me. Somebody would mention something to my mother or my mother would say to another person, "He would have been so-and-so today." These statements were always fairly guarded, as though it was assumed that I knew. But it was never explained to me. And I began to build up a picture of him. I always remember feeling that I must have been inferior to this other child, which is not logical, because this other child never really existed. In some way I hooked a supposed personality of this stillborn older brother on to a cousin who was just a few years older than me. I was often hearing about him from my parents. How wonderful he was. How good-looking. And how he did so well at school.

'I really wasn't that close to my parents. There wasn't much physical affection or even expressed affection, which is not to say that they didn't have feelings and I didn't have feelings. But these things were not shown. There was a sort of embarrassment about anything physical, even just what most people would regard as ordinary everyday hugs or touches. And I was particularly aloof from my father. There was this classic notion of what masculine identity is supposed to be about. I was no good at sport and all those things. He was always trying to persuade me to take up this or take up that or join the Scouts. I did some of those things just to appease him but they weren't really my thing. And of course this other brother would have been perfect, wouldn't he? He would have been the star centre-forward, playing for Arsenal. So there were all these ways in which I felt I was falling short in my parents' eyes. And I felt the other son would have been greater.

'That isn't to say that I didn't have any sense of identity myself, nor an awareness of what I regarded as my own achievements. It's just that I didn't think they were the things that my parents were particularly interested in. I was quite good at art and took one or two pieces home, but I don't think I ever showed them to my mother and father.'

Simon admitted to me that nobody in his family ever said anything to suggest that they were comparing him unfavourably with the kind of person his brother might have been had he lived. 'It was all in my head. I can see, with hindsight, that there was no way that my mother should possibly have imagined that the fact that she had had a stillborn child would affect me. And you see, essentially, it didn't. What affected me was the image I constructed, not the fact of his death. To give them their due, they probably had no idea what was going on. But when something is whispered or something is said in a way that you feel you shouldn't be hearing it – when there's a different tone of voice – you have the sense that there's much more to this than you know. I just picked up clues, if you like. And my creation was this paragon brother. I can see that secrets are often kept for the best of reasons and it's done with good intent. But, from my experience, sometimes it backfires.'

The shadow cast by a dead sibling also had a profound effect on Barbara Dorf, a witty and intelligent woman who introduced herself to me as somebody who didn't 'fit in'. By her own admission, she was 'a nasty child', conceived by her parents to replace their only son who had died a year before her birth. Now aged sixty, with a successful career as a painter, a circle of dear friends and a strong religious faith, Barbara has come to terms with her troubled upbringing in a household dominated by unhappy parents.

Their misery was projected onto the loss of the son on whom they had pinned so many hopes, but, as Barbara explained, 'They hadn't much capacity for happiness anyway. They were all right when they were having pleasure and throwing money around and going out, but they had little inner capacity for happiness.

'The thing was I don't think my parents really wanted children at all. They'd married in 1918 and, in about 1923, there was my sister. Apparently, they'd had the whole bedroom done out in pale blue, in the confident expectation it would be the adored son. But Mother Nature – she didn't do it for Henry VIII, she didn't do it for the Duke of Norfolk. She will do what she wants to do. It was a girl. I don't know what sort of childhood my sister had, because she has different accounts every time she speaks of it. But everything started to go wrong, the money started to disappear the way it did in the Thirties, the marriage started to go wrong.'

Barbara's parents seemed to believe that all their troubles would be resolved if only they could have a son. 'Well, when my sister was ten, there was a son. Mother endured a terrible pregnancy. The son only survived about three days. Then they had another replacement baby, which was me. My mother never got over it. It wasn't that she couldn't relate to daughters, she couldn't relate to any women. She had no friends at all while I was growing up. And my sister was terribly bitter, because she believed she'd have been a nice little girl if she'd had a little brother. Of course, I'm talking about a very, very long time ago. I was never told. One wouldn't have been told in those days; one wouldn't have been told any facts of life; one wouldn't have been told if one was adopted. It only sort of leaked out by hints. And there was some odd reason why my mother kept this terrible anniversary. She kept his layette in a special drawer and all the letters of congratulation. She kept everything in lavender.

'I was finally told, with great solemnity, when I was fifteen. I'd known anyway. I'd thought perhaps it explained why my parents were always miserable. It's interesting, because in the Twenties middle-class people lived very well. They didn't have to be rich. Labour was very cheap. Single families lived in huge houses. Buying silver and jewellery was nothing. Mother was always moaning that they'd lost their money and it seemed that losing my infant brother was no more real than losing money. My father used to bring mother extravagant gifts that weren't paid for, so of course somebody used to have to come and collect them. My brother seemed to come under that heading. There were so many things that were delivered to the house that had to be reclaimed anyway, it might as well have been the baby brother.

'My mother had built up a picture of what he might have been. He'd have been the perfect child, he'd have been Yehudi Menuhin, Paderewski, Lord Rothschild, everything. If he'd lived, everything would have been lovely. God knows what would have happened to him emotionally if he'd have survived, he'd have been a wreck. And my mother's misery wasn't of the retiring kind. She used to get into violent and unpredictable tempers. It was odd because she was rather a small, dainty person. If she was frustrated she used to scream and cry and it was the most horrible sound I've ever heard. The recordings you hear of people in the war zones of Banja Luka, Sarajevo, Mostar, are nothing on that terrible noise. It used to shut up everybody. Yet of course she could be charming when it suited her.'

Perhaps if her mother's behaviour had been less violent, perhaps if she had been able to show some real concern for her younger daughter, Barbara might have been able to feel some sympathy for the loss of her brother, even some compassion.

'But she demanded it. And my instinct told me that nothing could make her feel better. I'm dreadfully sorry, I don't want people to lose children, but there's not a darned thing you can do about it. I mean, what could I have done? I always felt my mother was one of those people who, whatever sympathy you gave her wasn't enough. My father – I don't know if the loss affected him as keenly as my mother – but it suited him to trade on it and whine. He was always very disturbed anyway. And I was always being blamed because I was so naughty. But you see children are selfish. If they're being told what to do by adults who've made a mess of their own life, then of course they're rebellious. They think, "What in the name of heaven is going on? This person can't manage their own life, why should they try and manage mine?" It was a question of survival. My brother had died before I was born. I wasn't responsible for it. But they never got over it.'

Barbara explained that her mother's background was mostly Jewish Slavonic. 'They were nothing like sentimental Gentiles' fantasies of Jewish families. There was no reason why they should have been. They couldn't give support and comfort, not being the type to do so and, in any case, were too exhausted by two world wars and a depression. My maternal grandmother was the worst of the lot. She liked to manipulate, to stir things up. Her system needed it. The trouble is the whole thing was so irregular. They were kind to me in lots of ways, but it was erratic. No, there was nobody I felt I could turn to. That's why I became rather a loner. I felt completely isolated most of the time. I never got on with my sister and I could do nothing with my mother. I used to get terribly miserable and introverted and frustrated and unhappy. Yet I was prescient. I could foretell things and still can. And, yes, I was a nasty child. It would be grossly dishonest of me to deny that. I was nasty because they were nasty to me. They were nasty to me because I was nasty. It was a complete vicious circle.'

When Barbara was about ten her father left her mother and went to work abroad. Her sister had been engaged but her fiancé had been killed in the Second World War. 'So there I was, stuck with these two dreadfully unhappy, embittered women. Before that my father and mother were always quarrelling and I couldn't understand, when my father left us, why she was even more unhappy. I thought she ought to have been pleased. With the brute selfishness of a child I thought she ought to be all right.'

The lack of stability in her family caused Barbara to look elsewhere for comfort. 'When I was growing up I used to fix on people, role models as they say nowadays. I did that with one family and they got bored and fed up and told me so in no uncertain terms. They weren't very nice about it. From the word go I wasn't a fit-in child. I never got on with other children very well. I wanted to fit in, every child does. I don't believe those who say they don't. I suppose I wanted to be the jolliest girl in the team and the leader of the gang.'

Later, as a student at the Slade, Barbara was still a loner. However, her observations of her own mother's lack of friends had taught Barbara some useful lessons. 'I've got a vast circle of friends now, because I realized one has to work at these things. One wants support, one's got to give it in return. I do all I can for them. I must support others. That's my prayer every night: "Most dear and merciful Lord, allow me always to support others." The friendships built up very, very slowly. And it was a salutary lesson, I mean, because it didn't come easily. I still may have no great capacity for happiness, but I've an interesting and amusing life with lots of fascinating friends.'

Before her mother died, when Barbara was fifty, the relationship between them had improved slightly. Her mother was still inclined to be critical and petulant, accusing Barbara of being neurotic because she was single, telling her not to wear 'those awful clothes', then complaining about her spending all her money on nice ones. By then Barbara was more able to deal with it.

'I knew that whatever I'd done wouldn't have pleased her. Eventually I did come to terms with that. I used to say, "OK, Ma, it would have been different if I'd have been different, but I'm just a little tired of this." When I got a lectureship in Oxford she was proud of me. And when I gradually started to show at the Royal Academy she became more mellow. Right to the end I used to look after her. I was determined to keep her in her own home to the end and fortunately she died in her own bed.'

It was then that Barbara was able to lay to rest, at last, the ghost of her dead brother. 'When the poor old lady died we cremated her with his clothes and all the letters. I just wanted rid of them. I said, "Let her take him with her into the eternal protection of the Lord." Of course I'm still affected in one central way. I've never wanted children. It's all too much pain and disappointment. Oddly, I can sense women who have had sons. They carry a distinct air about them.'

While both Simon and Barbara were free to talk about the experience of being born after the death of a sibling, in the case of the Dutch artist Vincent Van Gogh we can only speculate about the influence exerted from the grave by the brother who died exactly one year to the day before he was born. Van Gogh, the artist, was his parents' second child. Their first son was stillborn. He, too, was named Vincent. Not only that, but the first Vincent's grave was something of a shrine.

Our current thinking about personal growth and individuation makes the very idea of naming a child after a sibling who has died seem like asking for trouble. But in previous centuries, with their high infant mortality rates, it was not at all uncommon for parents to reuse the names given to children who had died for subsequent offspring. More than 140 years on from that birthday on 30 March 1853, which was also a death day, psychologists make much of the trauma attached to the young Vincent's regular Sunday visits to the churchyard, where his namesake's headstone marked the sadness of his brief existence, and of his parents' continuing distress at the loss of their first-born.

There have been many psychological studies of the tortured artist, who finally took his own life at the age of thirty-eight, and many biographers who have explored in some detail the effect on Vincent Van Gogh in his formative years of knowing he was something of a replacement for that first Vincent.

Let us close this chapter with an excerpt from just one of them:

> In his case, too, there was also the dead, immortalised infant in the church graveyard casting its longer and longer shadow, never to be forgotten because it bore his name. The whole thrust of his growth was in a sense entangled with this image, which could be seen as the corpse of his hope.[1]

NOTE

1. Philip Callow, *Vincent Van Gogh: A Life*. Allison & Busby, 1990.

CHAPTER 5
The scapegoat

Whatever the problems encountered by children born after their parents have lost another child, there is, at least, no sudden alteration of the status quo. The sibling's death has already made its mark. The children following on may perceive themselves as trailing in its wake or construct fantasies about it, but they will have been spared the whole business of witnessing their parents' immediate reaction to the bereavement and having to adjust to its aftermath. As we have already seen from June Wilde's recollections (Chapter 3), the way in which parents respond to losing a child has a powerful effect on the surviving siblings.

The child's need to grieve and mourn is an important part of reassembling the family into a healthy unit. Later, I shall be looking more closely at the ways in which children may be helped to work through this process. But, for the moment, let us look at a family bereaved of a child, in which not only was there little space for the remaining children to mourn, but one of the children became the scapegoat for her mother's anger. As Betty Rathbone told me, 'Grief is a part of anger and anyone who's full of anger may discharge it on to the nearest available object. This may well be the next child.'

Alice McKee is in her thirties and training to be a counsellor. Her interest in the counselling movement stems from the time she herself spent in therapy trying to unravel the pain and confusion which had marred her young life and early adulthood. She was six years old and her younger sister Sally was three when their older sister Lizzie died after falling off a horse at the age of seven. Their mother told them that Lizzie had been killed in an accident, but no further details were given and the two girls were sent to stay with some friends. Nor was Alice allowed to attend the funeral, although she can remember begging to be allowed to go.

'My father became very, very withdrawn. Lizzie had been his real favourite. He went to his room and didn't come out for days. He was in a desperate state. And we were all going round not talking. We didn't talk about it at all. Right from the beginning, any time that her name was mentioned there would be a frozen sort of feeling and you quickly changed the subject. When they were clearing out her clothes there was a dress that I really wanted, a little white dress with blue roses on it, but I wasn't allowed to have it. Sally got her teddy bear, but that was the only thing that was kept. And there was only one photograph that my father kept on a chest of drawers in his dressing room. It was as if she'd disappeared completely.'

Alice had been quite jealous of Lizzie having riding lessons. She herself had desperately wanted to learn to ride, but Lizzie, being the eldest, had been given first choice out of riding or ballet lessons. 'I felt it should have been me that died, because I should have been the one that was riding. I thought that for years and years.' Not only was there nobody with whom Alice could share her guilty feelings, there was also nobody paying any attention to the fact that her mother was becoming very violent.

'She started beating me very severely and she was always yelling at me. If anything went wrong in the house it was my fault. And because I felt so guilty I felt that it was right, that I really needed to be punished. I became very good and meek and I think this infuriated her and made her much worse. She was dreadful. Eventually it must have been noticed, because my father has told me since that she was sent to a psychiatrist for six months and that when she came back everything was all right. But that wasn't my perception. As far as I was concerned she was the same.'

When I asked Alice how it was that her father didn't realize that the ill-treatment was continuing, she said her mother became very secretive about it. 'After Lizzie's death he really cut himself off from the family. He just didn't want to face it. He's told me since that he didn't want to get involved in that way again because it was just so painful. He had to commute to London and he came back late. We only saw him at weekends. So I don't suppose he really did know what was going on at home.'

Two years after Lizzie's death another daughter was born and two years later Alice was sent to boarding-school. By then her mother had stopped hitting her, but the verbal abuse continued. I asked Alice if she had ever understood what was behind her mother's anger. 'Certainly, at the beginning I felt she was angry because Lizzie had died and not me. I felt she would have liked me to die. And, as we were growing up, Lizzie became this wonderful child. If Granny ever came and started talking about Lizzie she was always remembered as perfect. I felt it would have been much better if I had died instead and then they would have had this perfect child there.'

Although Alice loved boarding-school for the first year, her interest subsequently began to wane. She virtually stopped working at her lessons and spent much of her spare time drawing and writing stories. There was apparently no communication between the school and Alice's parents about her resistance to schoolwork. At home Alice spent most of her time reading in her room. 'Sometimes I would just sit. I would just sit until it got dark. Then somebody would yell from downstairs that it was mealtime and I would realize I was completely stiff and cold because of sitting. The only other thing I used to do was go for long walks with the dog on my own. So I was really very silent. I didn't talk to people among my family unless I had to. And I didn't have any friends at home.'

Alice left school at age fifteen with four O levels, and went on to do a year's secretarial course at her local college. It meant living at home again and she hated it. During that year she made a rather feeble attempt at killing herself one Sunday morning when her parents were out at a drinks party. 'I tried to cut my wrists with a razor blade, only I was afraid of cutting the tendons. I kept hacking away but the blood kept clotting. I soaked through a box of tissues, then I suddenly thought they would be back any minute and I'd better stop. So I just sort of bandaged myself up and wore a jumper. Then I realized I hadn't done the potatoes for lunch and knew there'd be trouble. So I had to rush down and put them on. Then we had roast beef. That was the worst bit really, watching this awful joint being cut. It was like me, it was disgusting. And I felt really sick and ill.'

Again, nobody in the family knew what was happening. Was Alice really trying to kill herself or was it a cry for help? 'Well, I'd written a very peculiar note to them, apologising and saying that it wasn't the fault of anybody. But, of course, I knew it was. Only I didn't want to say that. You see, I felt very sorry for myself. When I was a child I used to try desperately to please my mother. I wanted to get things right. By the time I was an adolescent I was no longer interested in getting things right, although I was frightened enough of her to still be very good, so perhaps I did think that by doing that she would be sorry. It might have been a cry for help, but I don't remember thinking that very logically at the time. I think I just wished I was dead really. But, anyway, I didn't tell anybody about it.'

It wasn't until many years later that Alice sought counselling; she went originally because of problems in her marriage. 'But then this other door opened. It was extraordinary. It took me the best part of a year to open that door. I wouldn't cry and I was always very polite.

Then I went away on holiday by myself for a week and I really missed my therapist. I was furious with her, but, really, all of that was about my mother. That was when it started. And at first it was all to do with my mother.'

Through counselling Alice was able, for the first time, to deal with the suppressed emotions connected with her childhood experience of being the butt of her mother's anger. In doing so, she found that she herself was very angry with her mother. It was like peeling the layers of an onion. Eventually she reached the point of recognizing how many buried feelings there were towards her dead sister, feelings which she had been carrying around inside her like a frozen lump for thirty years.

'It was an enormous relief to realize that Lizzie wasn't perfect. That was terrific. And to find out all the negative feelings I had about her and to be allowed to express them. And how angry with her I was. That was wonderful. All of that was really great, that I could get all of that out. And to know it was there even, let alone get it out. It took a long time and a lot of work, but it made me feel much stronger.'

Before she started her counselling sessions Alice had never spoken to either of her parents about Lizzie's death. When at last she broached the subject with her father she found that he would listen. 'And he told me a great deal. That was when he told me about my mother going to a psychiatrist. And he talked a lot about his feelings, how he went and shut himself off and why he did that. And we became a lot closer.'

Her mother was less approachable. The first time Alice tried to get her mother to talk about the events surrounding Lizzie's death, she claimed she couldn't remember anything that happened at the time. 'She just wouldn't be drawn out. But then I reached the point when I knew I must confront her, because I was still at her beck and call. She was still very much in control of me and I was still afraid of her.'

Alice decided to write a letter to her mother. She thought long and hard about what to say and how to say it. 'I wrote a letter really telling her how I felt about her, how I felt about what happened when Lizzie died, everything about what came later, right up to the present. I tried to acknowledge how terrible it must have been to have a daughter die and how crazy it would send anybody. I tried to acknowledge my part in it, especially as an adolescent, how I used silence as a weapon against her. I wanted to make that clear, because I knew she'd take it as accusatory. She didn't reply at all.'

For Alice, the lack of response was not important. What mattered was that she had stated her own case and regained some power for herself. She felt in control for the first time and really separate from her mother. The unravelling of her past also had a beneficial effect on Alice's relationship with her sister Sally. 'Nowadays I do talk to her. We have also talked about my mother . She has some memories too and she's been very helpful in pinning things down.'

Looking back at the actual events surrounding Lizzie's death, Alice said she felt that the only part of it which was all right was the way in which her mother broke the news. 'The trouble is it stops there. I think we shouldn't have been sent away. I think it would have been all right for us to see her cry, because then it would have been all right for us to cry. I think I should have been allowed photographs, I should have been allowed something of hers to keep. They should have talked about Lizzie. There should have been much more openness. I certainly would have liked to have gone to the funeral. I think that's so important. For years and years after she died I used to imagine that she wasn't really dead, that she was somehow mentally handicapped and had been put away in a home and that I would find her.'

Alice is still trying to resolve the conflicts of the past. 'In the last few months I have been coming to a deeper understanding of what it must be like to lose a child. I have tried to understand intellectually before, but this time it feels as though it comes from my heart. This has had an extraordinary effect on my relationship with my mother. It feels as though the deep resentments have slipped away and I can see her in a new light and with compassion. It all feels rather strange and new, but I feel full of hope at the possibility of a new relationship. I really do not think I would have come to this place if I had not been able to be angry with her first. The bad stuff had to be said to clear the way for something else to happen.'

CHAPTER 6
Never the same again

Alice McKee's belief that family life was never to be the same again after her sister's death was echoed many times by those I interviewed. No matter what the circumstances of the death, no matter how well or badly the mourning process was handled, those left behind felt the family was significantly altered. The death had been a turning point. Indeed, how could it be otherwise?

In some cases, that turning point brought positive as well as negative results. Take Susan T., who said, 'My sister's death at the age of nineteen, when I was fifteen, was a turning point in my personal development. Before then our parents demanded high academic standards. Her death released much more emotional contact and allowed other values to be appreciated. Her death jerked me out of what had gone before.'

That death happened nearly forty years ago. Susan, who is now in her fifties, works abroad most of the time as a teacher, returning frequently to England. She explained that, until the Christmas of 1955 when her sister Jane was involved in a horrific road accident, any outside observer would have thought that her family was a particularly fortunate one. There were five children: Jane, Susan, twelve-year-old Bridget, nine-year-old Richard and the 'afterthought', Charlotte, who was only a few months old. Her father was a successful businessman and the family lived in a large, elegant Georgian house, with a tennis court and orchard, in the relatively unspoilt outer suburbs of Manchester.

'However, in spite of the superficial and material well-being, the family would be described in modern sociological jargon as "dysfunctional". My mother was, and still is, a profoundly inhibited woman. She performed her domestic duties to perfection, but was unable to communicate affection or a sense of worth to her children. She also set impossibly high academic standards, which seemed to be her only criteria of approval.'

Susan recalled Jane in her younger years as a conventional, rather plain, child. She herself was neither of these things. Perhaps because of this she became a victim of Jane's 'endless spiteful bullying'. By the summer of 1955, however, there were signs of an improvement in the relationship between the two older girls. Jane had been at the Sorbonne in Paris and when she returned to England the two sisters met in London. 'All the old tensions had disappeared. Jane was suddenly chic and attractive. And, away from the parental pressure, we enjoyed a normal, relaxed, very happy few days together. It was the promise of a friendship which might have developed as we became adult, but, of course, was never realized.'

When they parted, Jane went to start her first term at St Andrews University, and Susan, with Bridget, went off to boarding-school in Berkshire. One Sunday, just before Christmas, Susan and Bridget were summoned to the headmistress's study and told 'with unexpected gentleness' that Jane had been injured in an accident while being driven back from Scotland. Susan was to go home, Bridget to remain at school. When asked for more details, the headmistress looked evasive and said Jane had suffered head injuries.

At home, Susan tried to make herself useful while her parents spent most of their time driving to and from Preston where Jane was in the intensive care unit of the local hospital. 'I remember trying to be helpful, unpacking her wrecked suitcase, which was full of broken glass, blood and carefully wrapped Christmas presents, and washing the blood-soaked duffle-coat she had been wearing.' On Christmas Day Susan went with her parents to see Jane for the first time since her accident. 'I was utterly shattered by what I saw. All my unfocused adolescent misery seemed nothing compared to the appalling physical wreckage that had been and still was my sister. Her head was shaved and her skull and face looked like a broken egg that had been clumsily pieced together with purple glue. I wept great wrenching sobs all the way home in the car.'

Her father, distraught at Susan's distress, explained that they had wanted her to see Jane when she was so much better than she had been immediately after the accident, when everyone, including the hospital staff, had thought she would die. Susan returned to school for the spring term and received a great deal of attention and kindness from both the staff and other girls. Jane had intensive brain surgery and, although blind in one eye, seemed to be recovering. 'The last time I saw her was in the private clinic in Manchester, sitting up, disfigured, very pale and fragile in a black dressing-gown, but managing to speak and looking forward to the future.'

In the Easter holidays Susan went to stay with her paternal

grandmother in Ireland and Bridget and Richard stayed with Irish cousins nearby, while their parents took Jane to Italy for a gentle holiday in the sunshine. 'It was a beautiful spring morning when my grandmother came into my room, weeping and saying over and over "Why wasn't it me?" Jane had suddenly lapsed into unconsciousness and had died in a hospital in Naples. The next few days are blurred, but I do remember sitting in the sun on the conservatory step looking at the sea, trying to grasp the finality of death. I remember sharing a room with Bridget that first night and really talking for the first time ever.'

In Naples her parents were experiencing 'a waking nightmare'. They appealed to the British Consul for help, only to be told it was not his problem. Jane was hurriedly buried in the Protestant cemetery in Naples and then the couple flew home, desperate to be reunited with their surviving children. It was an extraordinary reunion, an occasion for all members of the family to talk openly together for the first time.

'They met us – me, Bridget and Richard – off the boat at Liverpool and as we drove home they told us what had happened and how Jane would never have been entirely normal or able to have children. We shared the flood of letters, flowers and sympathy and I think it was a relief for my parents to be at home, supported by a return to something approaching normality. Charlotte, who was oblivious of the tragedy, was just walking and needed some serious attention after the last four months. It was a time when inhibitions were broken down and true affections expressed.

'For all of us it was a turning point. My father, who was a highly sensitive man, had behaved with great courage and care for the rest of us. But a couple of years afterwards he had a reactive depression and my parents' marriage went through a period of great stress. He had to take early retirement and I know the younger children suffered during the bad patch in my parents' marriage. But Bridget and I got closer. Before that our contact had been almost non-existent. Living in that large house, people could lose themselves, so there wasn't much contact between any of us.

'My parents never really got over it, not for a long time, if at all. And they definitely turned Jane into some sort of paragon. But, in a strange way, things in the family were better after Jane's death. I would say that her death had a profound effect and not an entirely negative one, at least for me. It sharpened my awareness of things. I grieved over Jane and still, after forty years, regret the waste of our relationship and how we briefly glimpsed what it could mean to be sisters. However, some of my burdens seemed to lift. A genuine grief seemed to drive out the introverted adolescent brooding. I started to make friends for the first time and to enjoy my academic work.'

Susan said that for a while after Jane's death, she felt she had to try to cheer up her parents: 'Then I think I just got on with my own life.' She was grateful that she was involved in the aftermath of the bereavement, because she thought this helped her to come to terms with it. But she regretted that the circumstances meant Jane was buried abroad and there was no chance for anyone other than her parents to take part in the service.

'It all happened in Italy. It was as if my parents wanted to leave it there and come home to their living children. It was a tragic and horrible time for them. They wanted to close the door on it. That was over and they wanted to get on with their other children and life. But I would have liked it if we could have had some sort of memorial service in England for the rest of the family and her friends. One day I definitely mean to visit her grave in Naples.'[1]

Another family in which the grief over the death of a child was shared openly was that of Anjana Dutta, daughter of an Indian father and an English mother. However, the circumstances leading up to her brother's death at the age of eleven had already taken their toll, for he had been born with a genetic defect and had not been expected to live for very long. Anjana, who is now twenty-eight and studying Chinese medicine in London, recalled that her brother's life and death had a powerful impact on her childhood. Until he died, her brother had been the main focus of her parents' attention; his death removed that focus, changing the structure of the family for ever.

The family was living in India when Anjana was born. She was the oldest, her brother was eighteen months younger and a baby sister was born when Anjana was eight years old. Although the little boy appeared to be normal at birth, it was soon clear that something was seriously wrong with him. Anjana's mother made frequent visits to the doctor to have her young son diagnosed and eventually, when he was two years old, she was told his life expectancy was five years.

'The illness was very much a progressive thing,' explained Anjana. 'When he was younger he was quite active and able to do a lot of things for himself. As he got older he started losing everything. He was going blind and deaf and was unable to walk. The whole family revolved round him. He was the primary reason that we moved to England, so that we could get help for him.' Although he needed almost constant care and attention, there was never any question of the family not looking after him themselves. 'My mother had been a nurse, so she was quite happy to take it all on and look after him. Her whole life was geared up around him. He was the complete focus of everything.'

Had Anjana found it difficult, with a disabled brother who was the centre of attention? 'I think at the time I didn't. That was all I knew. But when we moved to England I did find it hard because then I saw that lots of other families had a very different kind of life. Children that I was at primary school with would have family holidays. They would go camping and things like that. There was no way we could do any of that, particularly after my sister was born, because if we had to go anywhere I had to be responsible for my sister, while my mother was responsible for my brother. So it definitely made me very responsible at quite a young age, which I resented for quite a long time afterwards and probably still do. At the time I was just a very good girl and really helpful; I didn't rebel and I didn't kick up a fuss. But inside I was seething with anger about it and for quite a while I was really angry with my brother. I used to shout at him and argue with him constantly and pick on him.'

Then a few months before he died, her brother developed acute problems with his teeth and had to go into hospital to have them removed. 'While he was under the anaesthetic he stopped breathing. They had to resuscitate him three times and then he was in intensive care for about a week. But he survived and came through it. And I was very grateful because that really did force all of us to look at the fact that he was going to die, especially me because I'd been so horrible to him. If he had died then I think it would have been really traumatic for me because I'd had such a bad relationship with him for the last two years of his life. I was in a complete state. I just thought, "Please don't die, please don't die, because I haven't had time to mend the relationship." But as it was, I did. We did have another three or four months after that. That was the first time my mother talked to me, saying that he didn't have long to live. Before that I hadn't realized that he might die.'

Anjana found it very healing and helpful to re-establish a closer bond with her brother before he died. 'You see, when we were in India and it was just my brother and myself we actually got on very well. Also he was less disabled then. But later the animosity developed. I was angry because I thought he stopped us from doing things – well, he did. Life wasn't free. Maybe I would have fought with him anyway. And then at the stage when we weren't getting on there was a real tug of war with my sister in the middle. We both adored her and used to fight over her as well.'

I asked Anjana if her brother ever talked to her about dying. Her eyes filled with tears and she was unable to speak for several minutes. No, she said, he never talked about his own death. But she recalled that he had once opened up about his disability and she had found it profoundly moving. It was after their hopes had been raised by the possibility of a bone marrow transplant being carried out on the little boy. The whole family had been tested for their suitability as donors, but, sadly, none of them was.

'We were coming home on the bus and I can remember I was sitting next to my brother. This was at a time when we were fighting, not getting on, but I still felt quite bad that nothing could be done. And he was very quiet as well. And I said, "Are you sad?" And he said, "Yes, I'm sad, because now I won't ever be straight." That was his way of referring to his illness, saying that he was bent and he wanted to be straight. That's the only time I can remember him talking about it in a serious way. Before that he used to joke about it. But I never heard him talk about the fact that he was going to die.'

Recalling the day when her brother died, Anjana said she believed that he knew then that he was dying. Some relations had spent the day with them and, after they left, her brother, who'd been a bit sick all day, kept asking everyone to sit with him and talk to him. Then he started having convulsions and was rushed into hospital by ambulance, with both parents in attendance. 'My sister and I went to a neighbour's house and I just kept praying and praying that he wouldn't die. It seemed like my parents were gone for ages and ages. Then my Dad came back and just said, "I'm sorry." And I knew that my brother had died.

'We went back to our house. My Dad's a Hindu and he was praying. He was in a terrible state. Then we both went back to the hospital. My mother was still there and she thought I would want to see my brother. So I went to see him. I was really worried about how my sister would react – she was only four. When they told her he'd died she just said, "Oh, what are we going to do with his books and clothes?" There was no emotion there at all. Then she wanted to know exactly where he had gone and my father said, "He's gone to God." My brother was in the hospital morgue for a while and she went one day to see him. When she walked in and saw him lying there she said, "Oh, so this is God's house." It was really sweet.

'But it was really awful to see my parents grieving so much. I think maybe that was part of the Indian-ness. It's more open. The coffin was left open so that people could come and see. And that's why my Dad came to fetch me, because my mother thought it was important that I should see my brother, to see that he looked so peaceful and so happy and not in any pain any more. I found it very painful at the time, but I'm very glad she did that.'

However, in the aftermath of her brother's death, the whole structure of the family changed. 'My brother had been a sort of pivot in a way. After he died my mother had so much time on her hands. Without all the worry of looking after him, she wanted to do loads and loads more things. She went to college and became very active there, which then created huge problems between my parents because it really changed their relationship very much. And I think there was part of me that thought, when he died, "Well, now I can get a bit more attention." So I was quite resentful of the fact that instead of giving me more attention, my mother directed her energy outside. It felt like she suddenly had complete freedom to go for what she wanted to do, after having a life which revolved very much round the family and looking after my brother.

'From then on my parents' relationship went downhill completely and they separated about five years later. But I think that happens quite often, when a child dies, even if it isn't disabled. It's like a kind of anger with each other or they're both feeling so bad they can't comfort the other one. And I don't think they've worked through the mourning yet. I don't think either of them has ever really got over his life and death, both feeling responsible and helpless as well. My mother left home when I was about sixteen. I stayed with my Dad and my sister. I was very angry with her. I was very angry for quite a lot of the time. Our relationship has got quite a lot better in the last few years. We've talked about my brother. She told me she knew it was going to be a short life and she just wanted to make it a good life, happy and full and easy.

'I thought when my brother died that it wouldn't affect my little sister very much, but when she was about six she was given a balloon filled with helium and she lost it. And she was in a complete state, really upset, sobbing her heart out over this balloon. Then all the grief about losing our brother started coming out. It was all there. Locked in.'

As far as her own mourning process was concerned, Anjana found her school friends very supportive. 'I was off school for about two weeks and when I went back it was obvious that all of my class had been told, even though they didn't actually come right out and say it. But they were so nice to me and all the teachers were really nice. But nobody talked about it. I don't think I talked to anybody of my own age, but I did speak to my Mum and my aunt. And my mother still talks about him quite a lot, it's still very fresh in her mind. My father has photos up of my brother in his house, but he doesn't really talk about him much.

'I suppose the most profound effect of my brother's death was to make me aware that people do die. It's also made me and my sister very very close. I think that's one positive thing that has come out of losing our brother.'

NOTE

1. In August 1997, Susan and her two sisters took their mother to Italy, where they held a short memorial service at Jane's grave in Naples.

CHAPTER 7
Mother's comfort

It is invidious to measure out grief. Nor is it possible to make judgements about who suffers most when any one person dies. It all depends on so many factors. Yet it seems reasonable to suppose that the grief of parents for a dead child is very different from the grief of brothers or sisters for a dead sibling and that the parents will take longer to come to terms with their loss.

Betty Rathbone confirmed this. 'I think sometimes children are able to go through the grieving cycle faster than their parents. That is legitimate. But then you have a problem within the family in that the child has come to a resolution, is ready to get on with the rest of life, but has still got a parent who is very hung up on grieving. The implication of that is to try to make sure that the mother gets whatever help is necessary and for the child maybe to have to be extra patient because his or her needs are still not being met. After all, they're alive and they want parents to take an interest in what they're doing here and now. So I think, from the point of view of parents managing this, at the beginning they should openly grieve together, but later on it may be that the parent has to have a private weep, because the child has actually completed the process. And then it isn't appropriate for the parent to lumber them with the remains of their grief. They need to take that elsewhere.'

Annie Richards was fourteen when her older sister Marion died at the age of twenty, after being knocked off her bike. Although there were two other siblings – twenty-one-year-old Jeffrey and seventeen-year-old Sam – Annie was the one who became most involved with her mother's grieving process. Nearly ten years on from the accident, she still harbours some anger about the way in which she feels she was left to support her mother virtually single-handed.

In the immediate aftermath of Marion's death everybody rallied round Annie's mother, but within a matter of weeks that support had ebbed away. 'Nobody ever came round because they knew my Mum would get upset and they didn't want to hear it again, which was fair enough. But I didn't have any choice. I had to get home at the end of the day. After a certain amount of time I sometimes wanted to talk about my sister and not have it be floods of tears. I just wanted to talk about her. And my Mum couldn't do that. For a long time afterwards it would always be that she was crying, crying, crying. And I'd feel quite guilty if I did go out with my friends. When I came home I knew that if she wasn't crying when I walked through the door she had been five minutes before.'

Annie had been caught up in the events surrounding Marion's accident right from the start. At that time she and Sam were both living at home with their mother, who had been separated from their father for ten years. Both Marion and Jeffrey were away at university. One night the family had a telephone call from the police to say that Marion had been involved in a serious accident. An uncle drove Annie and her mother straight to the hospital – a journey of some 250 miles. It was hoped that Marion, although critically injured, would survive, but she died quite suddenly at dawn on the second morning after the accident.

'That whole time is still really vivid in my head. Right from that point I was at the centre of things, but at the same time I felt completely powerless in the whole situation. I remember feeling really patronized in the hospital when things were being explained to my Mum and they were saying to her – about me – "Does she understand?" I think I was seen very much as a child. And I found that hard.

'My family are close in times of crisis – or think they are. Everybody turns up, anyway. The whole extended family got involved. As soon as we got home they were all there in the house. There always seemed to be crowds of people about. I don't think I felt very much part of it because I chose to go back to school. It was half-term when the accident happened and I'd only had one day off after that. I really don't know why I wanted to go back. Nobody said anything to me, one way or the other. I think I just felt it would be easier if I was at school. But I have felt, since then, that I really missed out by not being around more, because other people, like my eldest brother, took time off work and they were all at home. They planned the funeral and I didn't get involved in that. I went to the funeral and we did have a song I'd chosen, but I think I could have been a lot more involved and I wish I had been. Marion was cremated, and my Mum made the decision that there wasn't going to be a commemorative rose-bush or anything like that. I didn't think I had a right to say anything. But since then I've really wished there was something somewhere that I could just go to. At the time, though, I just felt completely out of my depth.'

Annie recalled that she had cried quite openly at the hospital and on the way home. After that she took to crying on her own in bed at night, rather than letting other people see her tears. She said she was shocked at seeing adults cry, particularly her father. 'It was their kind of crying, so powerful and abandoned and out of control. I was used to having older, capable people around me. Suddenly they didn't look like that any more. I started to comfort them, rather than letting them see me cry.' It was a heavy burden for a fourteen-year-old and one which became increasingly weighty as the months went on.

'I think I definitely felt responsible for trying to cheer my Mum up right from the start. Everyone gave her the lead role. She was the person that everyone was concerned about and asked about. I remember thinking how terrible it was for her and that I'd got to get it right and be there when she needed me. I don't want to sound too harsh about my brothers, but I did feel very let down by them. My eldest brother came home for a couple of months after Marion died – he'd just finished his degree – and he was in the process of moving on to do a postgraduate course. So he just went away again and got on with his life. There were things he could have done that he just didn't do, like ringing home enough, or inviting my Mum up to stay or just being there. And he would never ask me how things were at home. Once I did ring him up and say, "Look, I need to come and stay with you for the weekend", and I went up determined to tell him that things were still really bad at home and it would help if he could be there more. But I just couldn't seem to do it; I had the whole weekend and I never said anything.

'My other brother was at home, but he was seventeen and could go out when he wanted to. And he did. He would go out in the evenings with his friends. So most of the time it was just Mum and me at home. And I felt that nobody, except me, really knew what was going on. I felt very lonely.'

I asked Annie whether she sought or was offered any help outside the home. 'The school was appalling. My friends were great, but that was in spite of the school. I was told by one of my friends that on the one day I took off they had an assembly and they were told that my sister had died and that they weren't to talk to me about it. So then they couldn't talk to me at all. What could they possibly say? "Have a good half-term?" So I felt completely strange, like an alien in the school. Some of the teachers were good. Some of them would say something to me and I would always much rather they said something, anything, no matter how crass it was. But when they didn't say anything and would look at me all the time through the course of a lesson, that was horrible. The first day I went back, the teacher who was supposed to be responsible for pastoral care called me out of registration into the corridor and said, "I'm very sorry to hear about your sister. But time will heal all wounds", and sent me back into the class-room. And that was it.'

During the year following Marion's death, Annie took quite a lot of time off school. On her report there was a note saying that her attendance could be improved. 'It didn't occur to them that there might be a reason I was taking time off. I think I became quite bitter about school. I felt I just wasn't respected as a person at all. This massive thing had happened to me and they were pretending not to notice, even though I must have been very different. There were times at school when I felt I needed somewhere to go in a moment of crisis, somewhere quiet where I could just be on my own for a few minutes. When you're an adult you can take that time for yourself, but in school your time is completely structured. So I just used to try and get out of school, one way or another.'

However, Annie did single out two people who, she sensed, would give her the support she needed. One was a teacher whom she liked very much, the other was Marion's best friend.

'They were very important to me, both of those people, quite amazingly so. I was so attached to them. If I could see them it was a good day and if I couldn't everything seemed ten times harder. I think it's probably really important for young people and children to be able to choose for themselves the person they want to talk to in these situations, because it might not necessarily be the most obvious person to everyone else. My sister's best friend seemed to understand. I felt she was seeing my family as I was. She could see what was going on and we could talk about it. And I talked to her about my sister much more than I did with my family. There were things I needed to check with her. I wanted to know if she thought Marion really liked me. I wasn't sure. I loved Marion and I thought she loved me, but I wanted to know if she liked me. I couldn't ask my Mum a thing like that because she just got upset and cried a lot and said, "Of course. Of course." I wanted to ask someone who I thought would give me an honest answer.'

The teacher whom Annie approached was also a friend of the family. 'I was finding school extremely difficult, really, really hard. At the end of one school day I thought, "I've had a horrible day at school. I can't bear to be here, but I don't feel brave enough to go home yet. I don't know what to do." This particular teacher happened to be around so I went to see her. I remember I did it indirectly. I went to her and said I was worried about a friend. After that I used to talk to her a lot. But I was a bit worried about doing it because it felt like betraying my family. But the thing I was most worried about was my Mum and I couldn't talk to my Mum about that. She was my biggest worry for most of the time. I think if I hadn't had this teacher to talk to I would never have made it through school. I'm sure I would have dropped out. And I'm glad I didn't do that because it would have mucked things up. I'd always been quite academic and wanted to go to university. After Marion died I just carried on, as if I was on automatic pilot. Also, I was quite afraid of losing my grip on things, so I felt it was important to keep working. But it was hard. I had those two people to talk to, but sometimes I wanted someone to *do* something about the way things were at home.'

Eventually the home situation did improve. 'I think it was really bad for about a year. I can't remember when my Mum changed, but she definitely did. And I think I got better at dealing with it. There was definitely a point when I was just sick to death of it, sick of the way she was so sad. I couldn't bear it. And then I knew I wasn't being a help to her, being there, so I would just stay in my room. If we ever talk about that time now my Mum gets very upset. I think she feels really guilty and I don't want that at all. She says she shouldn't have put so much on me and she feels bad about it. I just say, "That's all right, Mum. It was a terrible time. That was just the way things were." But it means we've never had a proper conversation about it. And she still won't admit that other people weren't much help. I feel there's this big pretence in my family that everyone is so open and supportive. I can still get quite angry about that.'

Annie said that, although she found the aftermath of the bereavement very painful and difficult, she believed she had managed to work through a great deal of the mourning process because, to a great extent, the circumstances at home forced her to confront it. She was less confident about her father and older brother.

'My father has never been good with emotions. He never talks much at all and I'd never seen him cry until Marion died. Then he cried a lot. And at that time he suddenly said how he felt there were ten wasted years of my sister's life when he wasn't involved with her at all. There were little glimpses of the terrible pain he felt about it all during these crying fits. Then suddenly it was all gone again. He's had depressions since about a year after her death. I don't think he's sorted out much at all. And I don't think Jeffrey did much grieving at all and it's mucking up his life now. He's a workaholic. He never gives himself time to stop and think. He drinks too much and then he gets upset and cries about Marion. I'm not sure about Sam. He's always been a very private, separate person. He went out with his friends a lot at the time and I think they must have been quite a lot of support to him. He's the person I can talk to most now about Marion, without being afraid that he's going to get upset.'

Despite, or perhaps because of, that terrible grief-ridden year, Annie felt that the bond with her mother was strengthened after Marion's death. She appreciated the fact that her mother kept a lot of Marion's possessions about the house and also let her have some of her sister's clothes. 'We were about the same size. I used to like to wear something of hers. It felt warm and comforting. There came a time when I didn't want to wear her clothes any more, but immediately afterwards it was really nice.'

She also admired the way her mother 'let go' of her when the time came for her to go to university. 'Right from when my sister died she became very over-protective of me. If we had to be apart for a weekend she would get upset saying goodbye. So when I was going away to university it was very hard for her. I know she realized she had to let me go and she was very good about it. My first term away I got a stack of letters from her and she phoned all the time. My sister had died in her second year at university and I found my second year very hard. I think it was guilt that I was going to get past the point where she had died. I was going to get older than her. I was going to get a degree. But I was also scared that something might happen to me. It felt good to get past that time. I felt quite relieved. And since then I've felt much calmer, more in control.'

The loss of her sister is still a matter of great sadness to Annie. 'My relationship with her was always stormy. She was very bossy, very much the older sister. But the last couple of holidays when she'd been at home from university we had started to be friends a bit more. She would ask me things about my life and I felt she understood what I was talking about. I'd just got that. And then it was gone. I feel I was robbed of all those things, that I'll never know if we would have ended up really good friends.'

CHAPTER 8
The parental dilemma

The role of parents bereaved of a child, and then having to deal with their surviving siblings, is extraordinarily difficult. Yet surprisingly, in these days of support groups for victims of just about every possible calamity, there seems to be little acknowledgement or understanding of this most painful and appalling situation.

During the course of my research for this book I met few bereaved siblings who were not critical of at least some aspects of their parents' behaviour in the aftermath of the bereavement. Parents too, with hindsight, could see that they had mishandled some of the crucial stages of the mourning process. Many of those siblings, now grown to maturity and, perhaps, parents themselves, could understand something of their parents' ordeal and feel compassion for their plight. As adults, they could recognize that their parents had been too shocked, too distraught, too absorbed in their own grief to fully appreciate the needs of their remaining children. At the time, however, these unhappy siblings had suffered in silence.

Few writers on bereavement have turned their attention to the post-death traumas experienced by children who have lost a brother or sister. One who has, Harriet Sarnoff Schiff, recognizes the importance of helping children through such a bereavement, although in the book she wrote after the death of her ten-year-old son,[1] she admits that she made mistakes:

> Parenthood now becomes walking and talking and listening and hearing someone else at a time when it takes everything just to think and function for oneself. . . . When Robby died, our instinctive thought was to get home and be with our children who had been left in the care of family. . . . We felt our children needed us. . . . We were right. They did.
>
> But six years later, our son, who was twelve when his brother died, remembers feeling unloved and alone during the entire grieving period and indeed for several years thereafter.

From her own experience she advises,

> At the time a child dies, surviving children must become the uppermost concern – almost beyond a parent's own grief. . . . It requires an enormous strength to deal with others' hurts at such a time, but it is important not to let a living child feel alone. Use any reserve you have to take time through the initial grieving process to switch roles from the comforted to the comforter. . . . The need for your individual attention is great.

The effect of bereavement on children was studied by Sula Wolff in her work on children under stress.[2] She writes, primarily, of the loss of a parent, but her conclusions are applicable here:

> There is evidence that the harmful effects of bereavement are more often due to its long-term social and psychological causes and to the emotional reactions of the surviving parent than to the impact of the death itself upon the child. . . .
>
> The belief that children are 'too young to understand' is often used to explain two common but contradictory approaches to life-and-death matters affecting children. Children are either regarded as insensitive, unable to take in anything of what happens, and therefore allowed to witness adult emotions and interactions without being given appropriate explanations. Alternatively they are endowed with exquisite sensitivity and vulnerability so that the facts of life must be carefully hidden from them.
>
> Only when parents are helped to master their own conflicting feelings in the face of death will they be able to adopt realistic and helpful attitudes towards their children.

Undoubtedly, the important word here is 'help'. Even the most aware and caring parents cannot always muster the necessary energy and concern for their surviving children and will need all the help they can get. Apart from leaning on relatives and friends, where else can bereaved parents go for support? And where can they get help for their children?

I spoke to two women who became involved with the work of The Compassionate Friends after they each lost a child. This is an international organization of bereaved parents set up to act as a support group for other bereaved parents. Initially, the emphasis was very much on helping the parents, but, more recently, the organization has extended its range to take account of the needs of bereaved siblings.

In 1992 it started publishing *SIBBS (Support in Bereavement for*

Brothers and Sisters), a regular newsletter for young people. It is written and produced by bereaved siblings themselves 'to provide a place where personal experience and information can be shared, and where the deep pain of grief is not taboo'.[3]

For Hazel Thomas, who runs a local branch of The Compassionate Friends, the introduction of *SIBBS* was long overdue. She joined the organization some time after the death of her eldest son Ross in a motor cycle accident just two weeks before his eighteenth birthday. A strong, motherly woman, Hazel had been through some chilling experiences with two of her remaining three children before she became involved with The Compassionate Friends. She had been at her wits' end about where to turn for help. Joining the group gave her some very welcome understanding of and support for her own grief, but, even so, her main concern was not only for her own children, but for the offspring of other members too.

'Ever since I belonged to The Compassionate Friends I have been more concerned about the children. I've been battling to form a group for them. I just want them to get together, as the adults do, because I know that if they do meet and start talking to each other it has to be beneficial.'

Although Hazel has met with some opposition in her attempts to bring bereaved siblings into The Compassionate Friends on a regular basis, she has made some headway. One of her first ventures, a barbecue at her home for fellow members and their children, proved a great success. She has also started a pen-pal scheme for the children and encourages them to meet each other and talk together.

Hazel's great concern for children who are bereaved of a brother or sister stems from the experiences in her own family after her son was killed. When I talked to her it was four years since Ross's death, but the events surrounding it and the terrible aftermath were still very fresh in her mind.

Ross was Hazel's eldest son. At the time of his death his brothers Neil and Dale were aged fifteen and thirteen respectively and his sister Lorna was eight. When the accident happened, Hazel was out walking her dogs prior to going to a parents' evening at Dale's school. She had left Ross at home and, when she heard an ambulance going past as she returned to the house, her first thought was for Dale, who by then should have been on his way to his Army Cadets meeting. By the time she reached home her husband was just coming in from work and, as she walked in through the back door, Neil burst in through the front door saying that Ross had been involved in a serious accident.

Hazel and her husband rushed to the scene. Ross had already been taken away by ambulance and the police told them to go home and wait for news. At home they paced up and down for more than two hours, before the police arrived with the news that Ross was dead. He had, in fact, died immediately after crashing his motorbike. They then received a telephone call from a neighbour, asking them to go and fetch Neil who had been seen walking up and down the road where the accident had happened, in a complete daze. Hazel's husband went to fetch Neil. Meanwhile, a friend who had heard about the tragedy rang to offer to look after the three remaining children.

Dale was still at his Army Cadets meeting and not due home for another hour. Hazel was persuaded to leave him there for the time being. 'That was my first mistake, agreeing to that. I bitterly regretted it later, because the man in charge there told Dale there had been "some problem" at home and said he must go straight home and not talk to anybody on the way. So Dale got in a panic. By the time he got home we had left to go and identify the body. The friend who was going to look after them was waiting, and when Dale walked in Lorna told him Ross was dead – just like that.'

Neil, Dale and Lorna were then taken to the friend's house. 'They were just bundled out of the way. I didn't realize until afterwards that Dale didn't know the whole story of how his brother died. He became more and more withdrawn during the summer holidays and when he started going back to school again he was in a really bad state. He became really suicidal. He was crying all the time. I could hear him sobbing and sobbing at night and I knew he wasn't sleeping. He could hardly move he was so tired. Well, we were all very lethargic – grief really does take it out of you.'

One day, as Hazel was walking past Dale's bedroom, she caught a glimpse of him through the glass panel in the door. He was standing on his bed pinning a poster to the wall, but in her anxious state she thought he had hanged himself. 'I got such a fright. And then I started panicking. I thought, "What can I do? Who can I turn to to help me with this?" I just didn't know how to handle it myself.'

However, her attempts to get help only stirred up more distress. First, she approached a married couple who were working as counsellors in her home town, but they refused to take on Dale on the grounds that they were trained to deal with adults, not children. They suggested she should ask the local vicar but he also declined, on the same grounds. Then a friend told her of a special unit for disturbed children, run by the National Health Service. Youngsters had to be referred by their GP, so Hazel made an appointment for herself with her family doctor and went to tell him the whole story of Dale's behaviour and her fears for him. It was arranged that the doctor should then see Dale himself.

'The first thing the doctor said to him was, "Well, Dale, what's all this your Mum's telling me about you wanting to commit suicide?" Then it was, "What a stupid thing to do. How do you feel about your brother? Do you feel sad about your brother?" I thought, "Bloody hell", and I could see Dale looking at me as if I'd blabbed out all his secrets. I felt he wasn't going to trust me any more. The doctor was very severe and in the end Dale started crying. It was a terrific ordeal for him, he's such a private person. I really felt as if I'd stabbed the knife into him, doing that. I felt so horrified by it that I never tried again. That was it. I became very protective of Dale – and all my family. If a counsellor had knocked on the door I wouldn't have let them in. I feel very angry that I wasn't helped when I needed it.'

Dale was a talented artist and one day Hazel happened to be flicking through one of his sketch pads. 'It was full of morbid death scenes. There was blood everywhere, dead bodies lying everywhere. The more I flicked through, I realized that each one didn't have a head. The head would be on the scene somewhere, but it would be on the other side of the road.' With this clue to what was actually going on in Dale's mind, Hazel chose to take him past the scene of Ross's accident on the way to school the next morning. 'I said to Dale, "Isn't it strange that, although Ross died over there, his motorbike came all this way and hit that lamp-post?" He said, "No, that's not what happened." Then I realized that he didn't really know what had happened. It seems that some kid at school had said, "Your brother broke his neck. That means his head was chopped off."

'Dale thought it was true. He thought Ross had smashed into the lamp-post and it had chopped his head off. What a dreadful thing for that poor little kid to have to live with. And that had been my second mistake, that I'd tried to protect him and hadn't taken him to see his brother in the funeral parlour. So then I was able to tell him how lovely Ross had looked lying in his coffin, just as if he was asleep. That there was no blood, it was all internal injuries. He'd envisaged all this blood and really horrific stuff. He hadn't asked me because he didn't want to upset me. He didn't feel I could talk about it and didn't feel he could talk about it. He was trying to protect me and I didn't realize what he was going through. So now I bitterly regret not taking him to see his brother.'

While all this was going on with Dale, Neil was becoming more and more withdrawn. 'You couldn't cuddle him, you couldn't talk to him. It was as if he'd built a wall round himself. He was so tense the whole time; when you tried to cuddle him he was rigid. In the end he had a row with his girl-friend and totally cracked up. And out poured all this grief for Ross.'

Hazel had, in fact, taken Neil to see Ross's body, believing that it would give him the chance to have a good cry in private. But he didn't shed one tear. Later Hazel learned that the two brothers had discussed the possibility of dying young only two nights before the accident. Ross had declared that, if he had to die young, he would like to go with his motorbike because he loved it so much, and that if this happened Neil was not to cry for him. 'So, of course, Neil didn't cry. He told me later he felt he couldn't cry anyway because he felt as if he had a big hard lump in his stomach. He couldn't cry even if he wanted to.'

Neil's crisis, as Hazel described it, came more than three years after his brother died. It took the form of extremely self-destructive behaviour. First, he drank a whole bottle of whisky, then tried to cut his wrists with a razor blade. 'It happened at home and was obviously a cry for help because I was there. We sat up all night and we both cried and cried and cried. He had gone through agonies because other people had said, "Neil didn't even cry for his brother." He told me people had said he didn't even love his brother. But he said it was because he loved Ross so much that he couldn't cry.' Neil also told his mother that somebody else had told him, 'You're the eldest now. You've got to look after the family. You've got to be another Ross.' He had felt there was no way he could fulfil this role and had deliberately tried to be as unlike Ross as possible.

'If only he had told me at the time,' said Hazel. 'They were like chalk and cheese. I would never have asked him to try and be like Ross. This all came out that night. I thought we'd talked it all through. Then five nights later there was a knock at the door at about midnight and there was a group of kids asking me to go to the graveyard as Neil was there being "a bit funny". He'd broken this bottle and rammed it in both his wrists and he was lying on Ross's grave and letting the blood drip into it. As Neil's got older we've been able to talk about what happened. We realize now that it wasn't so much a suicide bid, it was more a turning the frustrated anger at Ross's death in on himself. He found that by wounding himself he helped to ease the anger and because he was in such distress anyway he didn't really feel the physical pain.

'All of my children were close to Ross. Each one of them had a special relationship with him and they each felt it severely in their own way. Lorna, for instance. Ross used to come in and get hold of her and chuck her up in the air and dance with her. For a long time Neil wouldn't go near her, wouldn't even speak to her. That was when he was trying not to be like Ross. Now he's very close to Lorna. It seems he had to go through that crisis to get back to being the Neil we knew before. And since he's recovered he's been able to help me in the work of caring for bereaved families. He's very good at helping to support the siblings. He has a real empathy for them.'

I asked Hazel if her husband had been involved in the children's grieving. 'No. He's carrying a lot of guilt because he helped Ross to buy the bike. He has ranted and raved. He's so volatile he just flares up at the slightest thing. It's like living with a volcano. Yet for the first month he was the perfect husband. He supported me. He was brilliant. After that his grief took over. He was so angry. He's been angry ever since. I feel I've been tiptoeing round to keep the peace. It's been a terrific strain. Basically, I've soldiered on on my own. However, I'm feeling more hopeful about my husband now, because I've managed to persuade him to seek medical help and he's been diagnosed as having post-traumatic stress syndrome. It was such a relief to learn that and he's about to start specialist treatment.'

With her increasing awareness of just how traumatic the death of a sibling can be, Hazel now makes a positive effort to be more open with her three remaining children. 'At first I was being so strong, coping with everybody else. If I felt the need to have a weep I'd do it in secret so as not to upset everybody. Then one day I suddenly thought, "When these children grow up they're going to think their mum never cried over their brother." I realized they needed to see me cry. They needed to see it's quite normal to cry.

'It's a natural instinct to protect your children. I think, though, we have to involve them more. I do now talk very openly to them. And I'm keeping a watch on Lorna. She seemed all right at the time. People told her that Ross was in heaven and she seemed to accept that. But recently she's started getting severe eczema and I do feel there's a connection.'

Meanwhile, Hazel is pressing on with her work with The Compassionate Friends, trying to get children included in some of the group's activities.

'With bereaved parents you are walking on eggshells. It's difficult if a couple have lost their only child, because it's too painful for them to see other people with their children. But I am trying to organize social events which children can come to and those who feel they can't face other people's children can choose not to come. In fact, when I had my barbecue a lot of them did turn up. But I know most people don't understand how it is for these children. I don't remember anybody being concerned about my children at all. After Ross died they would ask me how I was. But I don't think I've ever had anyone come and ask me how my children were.'

This lack of concern for surviving siblings was also experienced by another bereaved mother involved in the work of The Compassionate Friends. Patricia Robson lost her first daughter, Joanna, in a road accident in the autumn of 1978. At that time her only son David was thirteen. 'We've got an enormous number of friends,' she told me. 'Everybody was concerned for me and my husband. But nobody said anything about David. I didn't see this at the time, but, looking back now, I don't remember anybody, except my best friend, saying, "How's David?" '

Until Joanna's death, Patricia and her family had lived a happy and untroubled life in a quiet Norfolk village. The two children were very close. 'They had an incredible relationship. Their personalities were entirely different. Joanna was the extrovert and David was shy and very quiet. He hid behind her and let her do all the talking. He just adored her.'

On the day of the accident, Joanna drove to her job as a personal secretary in Norwich, David left for school and Patricia's husband Kenneth went to work in a nearby village. Patricia spent the morning at home, but after lunch she went with her husband to his office, where she was helping with some of the secretarial work. As they approached Kenneth's workplace, they saw one of his employees standing in the road waving to them. It appeared that Joanna had been involved in an accident. Patricia and Kenneth rushed to the hospital, where they were greeted by one of Patricia's friends, who, with her own daughter, had come across the scene of the accident in Norwich city centre. When she realized it was Joanna who had been knocked down, she had asked to be allowed to go with her in the ambulance. The police were also there. They told Patricia that Joanna was thought to have fractured her skull. There followed hours of waiting for news. The distraught parents were not allowed to see Joanna at first, but were persuaded to go home and return later.

In the meantime, the friend had offered to collect David from school and take him back to her house. Patricia discovered later that her son had been told merely that Joanna had been in an accident, but he wasn't to worry because she had probably only broken a leg. On their way back to the hospital, Patricia and Kenneth picked up David and took him to his paternal grandparents' house. 'I didn't know what he had been told. I think I just said that Joanna had had a bad accident. After that things just went from bad to worse. When we asked to see Joanna we were told she had been taken away for brain surgery. They said her condition had worsened. We were kept waiting and waiting. The next thing I remember is that we were sitting with her in the intensive care unit. She was on a life-support machine and her head was totally bandaged. Before that we had been approached about donating her kidneys. My husband and I looked at each other. We were in total shock. I think we must have agreed; well we did, obviously, because she'd carried a card.'

Patricia sat up with Joanna all night. Her friend's husband turned up to offer support and the two men went off to wait in a side room. 'My husband just couldn't handle being there. Some of that night is just a blur in my mind, but I remember thinking that things were going wrong and calling the nurse. She came and switched off the machine. Then it dawned on me that Joanna was being kept alive. It sounds very naive, saying it now, but up until then I just hadn't realized what was happening. It was a nightmare. I said to the nurse, "But my daughter's not breathing. Are you keeping her alive?" And she said, "You can change your mind, if you want to." I said, "What do you mean?" And she said, "She's being kept alive because they're coming from Cambridge and they'll be late because of the fog." Then she put the machine back on again. It was all to do with the organs.'

Patricia explained that the nurse in question was foreign and didn't understand English very well. (Since that night she has become actively involved in a support group which befriends and helps families of patients in intensive care.) 'I felt we were totally in the dark. Looking back, perhaps shock clouded all sorts of things. Well, you wouldn't be sitting there if you weren't in shock. You'd be going crazy. I sat with Joanna all night and held her hand. She was stone cold, this girl who was an absolute beauty and the love of my life. I'm not a Catholic, though I was brought up in a fairly High Church, and I just kept saying the "Hail Mary" over and over again. I never left her, except to go to the cloakroom, and my husband came in then to hold her hand.

'The next morning, at about half-past seven, a doctor came in and said, "It's all over." She was still on the machine, but they were then going to take her away. We walked out of the hospital alone. I can hear my footsteps now clicking down that corridor. It was the corridor of hell.' At that very moment her very best friend from Colchester, some sixty miles away, having heard news of the accident, was arriving at the hospital. Patricia and Kenneth, meanwhile, were on the way to break the news to David.

'But I didn't get there in time to tell him myself. My mother-in-law was not on the telephone and she had gone down to a phone-box to ring the hospital at about the time we left. She'd been told on the telephone and came back to her home screaming, "She's dead. Joanna's dead." And that is how my son found out. But I didn't know any of this at the time. We then had to go and tell my parents who lived just a short distance away. Meanwhile, my friend had arrived at my mother-in-law's. She told me later that David was just sitting there pulling his watch to bits. And all he said was, "These things happen to other people, don't they?" There was nobody really there for him at the time.'

The friend and her son, who was a mate of David's, stayed with the family for a week. The two boys were together at the funeral. Patricia heard later that David had cried once with his friend, but after the funeral he became more and more quiet and withdrawn. 'David was still my baby at that point. He'd been cosseted. He'd had an idyllic home life. Then suddenly, there he was with this mother who had become a total zombie. I was in deep shock. Prior to the accident, I would have a cup of tea and cake and biscuits ready for him after school. He'd come in and we'd have a cuddle. Then we'd sit down with a cup of tea and I'd listen to everything that had happened that day. After Joanna died I still did the same things. But I did them in slow motion. I would ask him about his day, but I wasn't listening. I still tried to hold him, but I was dead inside. My emotions were dead. The mother who was there before was somewhere else. When I look back on it now, I realize he must have been desperate.'

At Christmas his parents bought David a television set. 'That was a very big mistake. From then on he spent his time alone in his bedroom with the TV. I think he never really had a chance to grieve, to be allowed to grieve. Or perhaps he couldn't anyway.' For his mother's Christmas present David had bought a record by Mary O'Hara, not knowing that it contained tracks of songs they had sung at Joanna's funeral. When Patricia played it she went to pieces and collapsed on the floor in a fit of weeping. David came in and threatened to take the record back. 'He couldn't bear me crying. I look back now and see that from then on he wouldn't do anything that he thought would upset me.'

Anxious because their son seemed so alone, Patricia and Kenneth began to wonder if they should attempt to have another baby. They were advised against it by their doctor, who thought they wanted another child for the wrong reasons. He suggested they should wait for a couple of years. 'It was going to be a bit of a gamble, anyway. I was forty by then. But we discussed it with David. We included him in the decision. I needed his permission. I felt that had I not done so he would have felt he wasn't enough for us, that he was inadequate. We talked about adoption. And David said, "Why can't we have one of our own?" '

The new baby, Harriet, was born eighteen months after Joanna's death. While Patricia was in labour David waited in the hospital with his father and, once Harriet arrived, he was allowed into the ward straight away. It was David who went and ordered flowers to be sent with a card saying, 'To Mum on the birth of our baby. Love from David and Kenneth.' 'So I think perhaps we handled that bit right. The baby helped him enormously. He was suddenly the carer, instead of being cared for. He was the big brother, instead of being the little brother. He put his heart and soul into Harriet.'

Although the baby brought great happiness to the stricken family, Patricia was well aware that her arrival did not bring about any movement towards the release of David's buried feelings over the death of Joanna. 'Whenever Joanna's name was mentioned he either went out of the room or didn't react. To this day he cannot talk about her. I remember once when he was about sixteen and trying to decide which career to follow, he got very down in the dumps. I got quite cross with him and said, "What *is* the matter?" He said he thought he'd blocked out everything that had happened with Joanna. He couldn't remember anything. I think this has caused problems for him. He's suppressed his feelings, suppressed things that should come out. I've tried very hard to help him. I've got out letters that Joanna wrote. I once actually got him to look at one which was all about the fun those two had had. I said, "Let's talk about it now. It's a long time. She would be hurt if she thought you couldn't talk about her." His face tightened and he asked me to leave it. He said he'd dealt with it in the only way he knew how. So after all these years I can't open him up any further.

'He's married now and his wife is very understanding. He's very fortunate because I think she's helped him enormously. He has a photo of Joanna by his bed. It's the same one he always had by his bed as a boy, ever since she died. About four years ago his wife persuaded him to go with her to take flowers to Joanna's plaque at the crematorium gardens. And now, at each anniversary and birthday, they go there together. I think the effort to do this must be enormous and it's a big step forward.'

David was also always very supportive of Patricia's involvement with The Compassionate Friends, which she joined soon after Joanna died. On the two occasions when she had a break from the group because of other demands on her time and energy, he was concerned that she might be letting down all the people she was helping. Like Hazel Thomas, Patricia became particularly interested in the effect of bereavement on siblings and encouraged the parents to talk about how their children were reacting. 'I was so concerned about David. It helped to talk to other parents. I wondered if David had reacted as he did because he was alone and had nobody to share it with. But I've learned that children in large families behave like that too.'

And what about Harriet? Did she feel like a replacement for Joanna? 'No, we very much guarded against this. We wouldn't have comparisons, although physically they are almost identical. I always had pictures of Joanna around the house and, from a tiny girl, Harriet knew who she was. But I had to try and make sure that Harriet wasn't affected by my grief. It was still there when she was born, eighteen months on. It doesn't go away. We also had to be careful not to turn Joanna into a saint. That can cause so much resentment. Harriet's growing up proud to be Joanna's sister and often says she wishes she had known her. I kept lots of Joanna's clothes and used to wear them myself sometimes. It was a comfort. Now Harriet wears them and she loves that. Having another baby wouldn't be everybody's choice. But to us it seemed the right answer.'

NOTES

1. Harriet Sarnoff Schiff, *The Bereaved Parent*. Souvenir Press, 1977.
2. Sula Wolff, *Children under Stress*. Penguin Books, 1969.
3. *SIBBS*, Spring 1992. The Compassionate Friends.

CHAPTER 9
The black sheep

How many parents can say they have never used the expression, 'They'll grow out of it' when they find their offspring going through some particularly tricky phase of development? Indeed, it can be quite a comforting thought. In the average family – if there is such a thing – most children do 'grow out of' some of the more tiresome stages which mark their progress from babyhood to adulthood. These predictable periods – for example, the toddler tantrums, the teenage rebellions – are well documented and there is plenty of advice available for parents who feel they need it.

However, the child whose family structure is shattered by the death of a sibling is going through a stage which is outside of the 'normal'. He or she is having to contend with emotions, changes and conflicts which even mature adults find difficult to deal with. Yet, there seems to be little written material which could give parents some understanding of what their children might be going through. Not surprisingly, many adults seem to hope or believe that young people caught up in such a tragedy will somehow get through it on their own, will 'grow out of it'. This is wishful thinking.

'In a grief situation I don't believe in spontaneous "growing out of it",' declared Betty Rathbone. 'If the child has had the luck to meet somebody who can help them come to terms with the situation – it doesn't necessarily have to be a professional – then they will grow through it. But it's not something that happens mysteriously. It happens from going through a process – the kind of process that we, as professionals, would try to pursue. This means allowing the child to express anger and regret and guilt. Children may well be carrying quite inappropriate guilt, because children are particularly egocentric. So that when something happens they tend to think it is their fault. Also, children are quite likely to have been angry enough at some point to have wished, quite literally, that so-and-so was dead. Most of the time those wishes are experienced as harmless because, of course, the person doesn't die. But, if the person does die, then with very young children, who are still in the stage of magical primitive thinking, they will have a tremendous load of guilt. "If only I hadn't been angry and wished they'd die, perhaps they'd still be here." I am talking particularly about the under-fives, but even children quite a bit older than that might be tipped into this way of looking at it. And an adolescent might very well get the thing out of proportion. Difficult grieving often starts with having had your last meeting with the person parting angrily. Of course that sort of thing can be true of people of any age, but the younger the child, the more likely they are to have difficulty in correcting that sort of faulty thinking without a great deal of help.'

Unexpressed guilt caused great distress and suffering to Francesca Blythe after the death of her favourite sister. She felt guilty because she was still alive and guilty because she felt it was her fault that her sister had died. Added to this burden of guilt was a whole range of painful feelings, none of which she was able to express at the time nor, indeed, for many years afterwards.

Francesca is now fifty. A single mother with a son in his twenties, she works as a welfare adviser for a large charity. She was thirteen when her sister Sadie died at the age of fifteen. In the years since then she has found it almost impossible to open up to anyone about her sister's death and the powerful effect it had on her. 'When my sister died it was never talked about afterwards,' she told me. 'There was no counselling available and we were expected to get over it quickly and get on with things. It still affects me, even now.'

As she shared her experiences with me, Francesca broke down and wept several times. As a girl, she said, she had never talked about Sadie's death. So when did she start talking about it, I asked her. 'I don't think I ever have. It's a hard thing to do. I sometimes think I have never been the same since. It was such a momentous event. And now I'm older I think about it more. I believe it set in motion a train of events that never really got sorted out. It was like the beginning of the end.'

The background to that 'momentous event' was a family of six children with a widowed mother who had buried her grief for the loss of her husband in a struggle to make ends meet. Francesca was the fifth child in the family, only fifteen months younger than Sadie. There were two much older sisters, an older brother, described by Francesca as 'shy and reclusive', and a baby brother, who had been born six months after their father died. Francesca was not at all close to the three older siblings, and felt very hostile to her younger brother who was their mother's favourite.

'She doted on him. He had been born prematurely and was very delicate. She preferred boys anyway; she didn't like girls very much. He turned into an absolute monster. If he couldn't get his own way he would just lie on the floor and scream. He was violent and used to attack us, but my mother seemed to have no boundaries or control of that. Sadie and I were treated as a pair in the family. We were dressed alike; we went off to boarding-school together; we played together; we even made up our own language so that nobody else could hear what we were talking about. I adored her. She was very bright, very clever and very pretty. She was easygoing and gentle, but she had a strong personality and everybody liked her. I was very different. I was always very restless and not as bright. I think my mother certainly found me quite difficult.'

Francesca explained that she had been sent to live with an uncle and aunt after her brother was born. She was with them for nearly two years until she was four years old and only went back to her own family after it was suggested that the uncle and aunt might adopt her permanently. 'My mother rushed up and got me back again. I think I found it very hard coming back to a very chaotic family situation from a very ordered life with my uncle and aunt. Everybody had got used to my not being there. And I was very jealous of my little brother having so much of my mother's attention. So Sadie and I ganged up. We were complete with each other. It was very much her and me against the whole family.'

At age eleven, Sadie won a scholarship to a day-school. Francesca failed to get a scholarship and was moved around from school to school, but the relationship between the two girls remained strong. Their mother was a freelance journalist and just managed to keep the family afloat, but money was always tight. 'I think she suffered terribly from her husband dying. We were very poor, like a lot of people in those days, and there were no benefits then or anything like that. She had to work all hours. She just couldn't cope with other people's feelings. I don't think she could cope with her own. I didn't have a good relationship with her and I never discussed anything personal with her.'

When Sadie's school announced that it was planning a trip to Switzerland for some of the pupils, there was no spare money to pay for it. 'So she got paper rounds and saved all her money for over a year to go on this school journey. Two weeks before she was due to set off she had appendicitis and went into the local hospital to have her appendix removed. When she came home she was devastated because she thought she wouldn't be allowed to go on the trip. Well, I was very close to her, as I said, and she used to show me her wound, which was seeping open. She'd say, "You're not to tell Mummy, because if she knows I won't be allowed to go." So I promised not to tell. And she pretended she was quite well. I don't know how she got away with it, but she did. And she went off to Switzerland with the other children. On her first day there she was rushed into hospital with peritonitis. I don't know the details, but poison from the wound or the appendix had got into her bloodstream. She was in the hospital for eight weeks and there was no question about it. She was going to die. My mother flew over to be with her, and my oldest sister, who was married and had a young baby, took in my younger brother and me.

'Nobody ever said what was happening. When I asked about Sadie I was told she'd be all right. But she died. My sister told me and my brother. He didn't respond at all, he just went off fishing. I was very upset, but nobody really said anything. My sister was buried in Switzerland and my mother came back two weeks later. She brought all my sister's clothes in a suitcase. I remember them being on the bed and asking if I could have them. I think I felt overwhelmed, because we didn't have many pretty clothes and she'd had new clothes for going away. It was a momentary thing, feeling we were practically the same size and thinking perhaps I could have them. It was all mixed up with grief for Sadie. My mother just hit the roof and said, "All you can think about is her clothes. If you'd died, she wouldn't have talked like that." And I had this terrible feeling that the wrong one had died. And I remember thinking that if I'd told them about Sadie's wound looking so dreadful she wouldn't have died. I can still remember that wound and Sadie begging me not to tell anyone.'

Taking her cue from her mother and the rest of the family, Francesca realized that there was to be no discussion of Sadie's death. Life had to go on, as if nothing had happened. "We all just clammed up. As time went on, I became more and more convinced that the whole family would have preferred it if I had gone. Sadie was an extraordinary person: clever, musical and artistic. I had no talents whatsoever. I always felt that I, who was so much trouble, so awkward and clumsy, should have been the one who died.

'After that I think I became very difficult indeed. I was terribly isolated in my teens. My older sisters had both left home, my older brother, who'd been at boarding-school, had gone to live and work in the country and my little brother was thoroughly unpleasant. I can remember being at school one day, when I was about fifteen, and in the art room we had Stanley knives. I made little prick marks with a knife up and down my arm. I was so unhappy. I felt I was not a very nice person. I went on doing that for over a year. I went through the most horrific teen years. Looking back now I think it's amazing I escaped getting into prostitution and drug addiction. Someone must have been watching over me, because I could easily have ended up in the criminal system.'

Throughout those painful years, the guilt over her sister's death persisted. 'I got Sadie's bedroom after she died and I was pleased about that. But there were terrible guilt feelings about having her nice bedroom, which I'd always coveted. I was so unhappy that she'd died, but I felt I should have more feelings of grief. I don't remember crying much at all. I don't remember talking to anyone at school about it. I missed Sadie for years and years and years. Sometimes now I think about her and wonder what she would have been like, whether she would have grown up to be the golden girl I thought she was. But I've never been able to talk about her with my mother.

'I think my mother could have done more to help us at the time. I think we should have all gone out there, for a start, but it was out of the question because we had no money. I do remember my older sister telling me that Sadie was in great pain in the hospital, so perhaps it would have been awful for us to see her. But I was the closest to her and wish I could have seen her. Now I'm older I can see that my mother is very limited emotionally. She provided for us, but I don't think she was able to give love and affection and warmth. But perhaps if she had had some support herself she could have given us more support. I know I'm very harsh on her, but I think now – and it's something I couldn't think at the time – that the death of your child must be the most horrific thing. It's the worst thing I can imagine. I also think we had enormous problems as a family. We were not emotionally close. We all did our own thing. None of us supported each other.'

More recently, Francesca has been able to talk about the past with her oldest sister and has found it helpful. But she still retains an underlying feeling of sadness. She said she cannot remember ever feeling really happy or contented with her life.

'I was a great reader. I guess that's how I probably dealt with the grieving. I used to read about five or six books a week. In those days they were all about schools and families. There was always Mum and Dad and a girl and a boy. That was my ideal. If you had that you were normal and all right. I've always had a dread of being seen as not normal. And I do feel "not normal" because I don't have a partner. I know many people don't have partners, but I feel one should. And I always wanted a large family, because I've always been very good with kids. That's why I went into teaching. I feel I've never really achieved very much. All my mother cared about was that we got married, which was strange for a career woman. I had my child without being married and I don't think she's ever forgiven me for that. I think it would have helped, years ago, if we'd had family therapy, all of us. As an adult, I've never had therapy or counselling. I think that's possibly something I may well do sometime. I think it might do some good to address my relationship with my mother, my sister's death, my relationship with men. I think these things need to be sorted out.'

CHAPTER 10
The avenging sister

As Francesca Blythe recognized, her sister's death was only a part, albeit a major one, of a complex set of family circumstances which influenced the way in which she grew up and how, as an adult, she now deals with life.

When it comes to a family as famous and as widely written about as the Brontës, it is not possible, within the framework of this book, to do more than touch on some of the key points concerning the effect of sibling bereavement within that family nor to concentrate on more than one of the four surviving children.

The novelist Charlotte Brontë was the third child in a family of five girls and one boy. After their mother died in 1821, when Charlotte was only five, the bonds between the siblings became exceptionally close. 'The children did not want society. To small infantine gaieties they were unaccustomed. They were all in all to each other. I do not suppose that there ever was a family more tenderly bound to each other,' wrote Charlotte's first biographer, Mrs Gaskell.[1]

Three years after their mother's death the two older girls, Maria and Elizabeth, were sent to Cowan Bridge, a school for the daughters of clergymen, where, before long, they were joined by Charlotte and Emily, the fifth child in the family. Within a year both Maria and Elizabeth were dead of consumption (as TB was known then), victims of the school's insanitary conditions and harsh regime. Thus Charlotte, as the oldest sibling, became something of a mother figure to the other three, Branwell, Emily and Anne.

She was a mere nine years old. Her personality had been perceived by one of the school's teachers as 'bright' but, according to Mrs Gaskell:

> I suspect that this year of 1825 was the last time it could ever be applied to her. . . . She remembered how anxiously her dear sister Maria had striven, in her grave earnest way, to be a tender helper and a counsellor to them all; and the duties that now fell upon her seemed almost like a legacy from the gentle little sufferer so lately dead.

Mrs Gaskell can be forgiven for her rather sentimental view of the heavy burden of responsibility thrust upon Charlotte at such a young age. As a close friend and admirer of the young writer, she saw it as her duty to honour Charlotte's memory. Inevitably, her own strict religious principles would also have coloured her assessment. Thus, there is this suggestion of a somewhat passive acceptance, but a girl of Charlotte's passionate nature must have had many difficult and painful emotions to contend with as she took on the role of the responsible oldest sister.

That she became extremely anxious about the health of her surviving siblings is clear from a later incident concerning Anne, who by then was a pupil at a school at Roe Head. Anne was taken ill, and Charlotte, an ex-pupil now employed as a teacher at the school, became very angry with the headmistress for not taking Anne's illness seriously enough.

> Miss Wooler considered it as little more than a common cold; but Charlotte felt every indication of incipient consumption as a stab at her heart, remembering Maria and Elizabeth. . . . Stung by anxiety for this little sister, she upbraided Miss Wooler for her fancied indifference to Anne's state of health. . . . About this time, she would turn sick and trembling at any sudden noise, and could hardly repress her screams when startled.

The fury she felt at the treatment which her two older sisters received at their school was later channelled into Charlotte's own writing. Readers of her first novel, the classic *Jane Eyre*, will be familiar with the account of the heroine's experiences at Lowood (Cowan Bridge, thinly disguised) and the tragic Helen Burns (Maria) who died there. As Mrs Gaskell explained, Charlotte became 'an unconsciously avenging sister of the sufferer'.

Mrs Gaskell also wrote of Charlotte's serious approach to life as having been the result of her sisters' deaths.

> I can well imagine that the grave serious composure, which, when I knew her, gave her face the dignity of an old Venetian portrait, was no acquisition of later years, but dated from that early age when she found herself in the position of an elder sister to motherless children.

Reflecting on some of Charlotte's correspondence with one of the close friends she made at the Roe Head school, the biographer was

> struck afresh by the absence of hope, which formed such a strong characteristic in Charlotte. . . . In afterlife, I was painfully impressed

with the fact, that Miss Brontë never dared to allow herself to look forward with hope; that she had no confidence in the future; and I thought, when I heard of the sorrowful years she had passed through, that it had been this pressure of grief which had crushed all buoyancy of expectation out of her . . . or perhaps the deep pang of losing her two elder sisters combined with a permanent state of bodily weakness in producing her hopelessness. If her trust in God had been less strong, she would have given way to unbounded anxiety, at many a period of her life.

During her research for the biography, Mrs Gaskell was given access by Charlotte's widower, the Reverend Arthur Bell Nicholls, to a parcel containing some of the dozens of tiny manuscripts – the miniature books of stories, poems, dramas and novels, each concerning the same characters – which the four surviving Brontës had written during the years following the deaths of Maria and Elizabeth. Mrs Gaskell used only a few extracts from these extraordinary compositions to indicate that Charlotte had shown signs of literary creativity from an early age. The biography was first published in 1857 and the manuscripts didn't surface again until nearly forty years later, when they were sold by the Revd Nicholls to the journalist Clement Shorter, who used them for his own publications about the Brontë family.

There have been many interpretations of these juvenile writings, but one of the most interesting and relevant to the theme of this book is that put forward by Margaret Lane:

> This highly complex creation, which took so strong a hold on their imagination that all four children passed their entire youth under its influence and even in maturity remained addicted to it like a drug, began in 1826. . . . The mature work of Charlotte and Emily cannot be fully understood without some knowledge of the play-sagas of their childhood, and the violent, long-drawn, uninhibited day-dream life to which these gave rise. . . . To sensitive natures dismayed by life – and it seems that the four of them were all, for different reasons, so dismayed – there is great comfort and great danger in the possession of an absorbing daydream in which to hide one's head. . . . Charlotte in maturity recognised the dangers of the dream and consciously broke out of it, though not without anguish, and not before it had conferred its curious bloom on her mind. . . . Emily stayed resolutely within it, like some self-communing votary in her cell, and by so doing achieved freedom for the development of her genius. . . . Branwell dwelt in the drug-like dream too long, taking refuge from his fears and secret inadequacies: on all of them its influence was profound.[2]

Ms Lane's view is entirely credible, but it is only speculation. The key players in the events, those four surviving children, bereft of their mother and with a father who kept his distance to a great extent, have left no subjective accounts of the effect of the sudden loss of the two older sisters who had been such an important part of the unusually close-knit sibling group. Even if they had done so, we can imagine that their views would not have been the same. Their individual temperaments, their own particular relationships with the two dead sisters, their different positions in the pecking order, all would have coloured their perceptions.

None the less, there seems to be every reason to suppose that those early sibling deaths made their mark on the survivors and shaped much of the content of their creative genius.

NOTES

1. Mrs Gaskell, *The Life of Charlotte Brontë*, first published 1857.
2. Margaret Lane, *The Brontë Story*. William Heinemann, 1953.

CHAPTER 11
Family structures

In the Introduction to the book, I explained my perception of how the death of my eldest daughter had affected her younger sister. I knew that the death had also had some impact on the three girls who were born later, so I asked all four of my surviving daughters if they would be willing to give their individual accounts of being in a family which had lost a sibling. None of us was quite sure what would emerge from these interviews, but I believe it has been helpful for them – and I know it has been profoundly thought-provoking to me – to focus, almost for the first time, on the many effects of that death.

The background to their accounts was the sudden death of Rosamund, my first child, at the age of three, from broncho-pneumonia which developed as she was recovering from measles. Lucy was fourteen months old at the time and my third daughter, Charlotte, was born nine weeks later. Emma arrived on Lucy's fourth birthday and Katy was born seventeen months after that. In order to simplify matters for the reader I asked my daughters, when relating their experiences, not to use personal pronouns when referring to me. This device seems to have been quite effective and has, I hope, made their accounts more accessible.

Lucy is now thirty and has a young daughter of her own. Until she was fifteen, she had no conscious recollection of Rosamund's death. She knew of her older sister's existence, but was not in touch with any memories of her. 'When I started remembering it was triggered by going into hospital in great pain to have my appendix out and being separated from my mother. There was a sense of desperation. My great fear was that I was going to die. When I came out of hospital I remember being very distressed and very insecure. I started using this very small baby voice. It came unbidden. I couldn't really control it. It was as if I was pretending to be a baby.

'One day my mother got very irritated by it and said, 'Oh Lucy, stop using that stupid voice." I remember saying, "You don't love me, you only love Rosamund", which was nothing to do with what had happened at that particular moment. My mum realized then that it was something to do with a deep distress. Then we had this very strange experience when everybody else in the family went out and we had some time together to look at what was going on. My mum felt that something needed to be explored and I trusted her judgement, but it felt extremely weird. Then all this stuff came out about being a baby when Rosamund died.

'After that I went and had counselling about it. It was all in there, all this stuff about Rosamund dying, being a baby, and then suddenly having another sister. From my viewpoint it seemed that the having of another sister almost eclipsed the loss of the big sister. It felt as if I'd had two families. I had a family that was Dad and Mum and Rosamund and me, then I had another family. It felt as if the change from the first family to the second happened overnight. I know it wasn't overnight, but my experience was that a swap was made. Suddenly there was no Rosamund, but Mum and Dad and me and Charlotte, then Emma, then Katy, this kind of accumulation of small children. In my romantic memory of it, it was always fabulous in my first family. The second family was crowded. I felt a sense of responsibility in it, being the eldest, and there was a deep unexplained resentment towards my other three sisters. I had assumed it was just because that's what older sisters feel like and I used to talk about it to friends who had little sisters and brothers. But for me there was an added element of feeling that it wasn't quite how things should be.'

Before Lucy got in touch with all those buried feelings associated with Rosamund's death, she had been aware of the fact that there had been an older sister. She had seen photographs of her and talked to her mother about her. 'As far as I remember, all the pictures of Rosamund were in a drawer, they weren't actually on view. My youngest sister and I spent a lot of time talking about her, but I don't remember talking to the other two very much. I remember when Emma was born on my fourth birthday my grandmother saying to me, "You've got to help your mother now because you're a big girl", and feeling, "No, I'm not. The big girl's not here." That was a very strong feeling and it came out later when I had the counselling. That was the strongest thing to start with, this enormous resentment that Rosamund had somehow clocked off and left me with the role she should have had. It was very difficult to have those feelings, very painful. It made me feel guilty, because she didn't do it deliberately, did she?

'I think I felt angry because she'd let me down. My counsellor was very good and she didn't judge at all. She talked about the process of mourning and its various stages and said there's always this stage of anger, followed by guilt, which then usually leads into the grieving, the sadness. But with me it's all been a bit disjointed, because I had the initial eruption when I was about fifteen, and a lot of that was about what I'd lost in terms of my family role. Then about four years ago, when I was pregnant, it started to hit me that I'd lost a person and I started to want to know what she'd been like. Now that I've got my own daughter it's even more touching. This is what Mum and Dad lost. I can't imagine the pain of that, losing a child.'

Lucy said she felt something inside her was impelling her through her counselling sessions. 'That experience leads me to the conclusion that things come into your consciousness when you're ready for them to, when you're strong enough to cope with them or when you know you've got the support around you. Partly, I was just really fascinated by the process. My counsellor said, "You, Lucy, at fourteen months, couldn't speak, but you had a lot to say. Now you can speak and what you need to do is to lend that little Lucy the power of communication so that she can be heard." It was a process of natural hypnosis. I can't remember all the details but I would somehow start talking in the voice of baby Lucy – that's what the counsellor and I called her – and it was as if I was an onlooker. It was very moving. It felt like a sort of journey to meet up with a real person who got lost underneath all this other stuff about being a grown-up "big" girl.

'To begin with it was just deep distress and lots of crying, which was a physical relief. It really was. The baby Lucy was afraid of losing Mum and wanting to know why Rosamund had gone and why was everyone so sad. And she was saying, "You've still got me, you've still got me." I don't think it would have come out if Rosamund had been a secret. I mean, I knew her name and I knew she'd died, although I couldn't remember her. It was such a short life and experienced by me from such a powerless place. The strangest thing is not knowing who she was. I remember having her Busy Lizzie doll. I don't know where it is now, but my Mum gave me a card that my sister gave me for my first birthday and I've still got that. It was extremely important to be given it, because what gets lost in all this is her relationship to me. Almost the most important thing about her is that she died. I find it difficult to say this, but it's as if her death outweighed her life. The memories of her are very shadowy and it's strange to miss someone you didn't know very well. If people ask me how many sisters I've got I always say four. I feel it's right to include her. I miss her particularly when important things happen to me. When my daughter was born I felt a very keen loss of a big sister. My other sisters were all there and it felt somehow that Rosamund should have been there too.'

I asked Lucy, from her experience, what advice she would offer to parents in a similar situation with such a young bereaved child. 'I think the main thing is not to hide it. To be open and not deny that you're grieving. I think the openness has to be balanced. Not pushing information but making it available if and when it is required. I think it would have been more difficult for me if the subject of Rosamund had been hush-hush. I mean, we could talk about her. But it would have been nice to have a photograph of her out somewhere. I do have photographs of her now, but I found it very difficult to ask for them because of not wanting to stir things up. I can't talk to my father without him getting really upset. I think it's still a source of enormous sadness which hasn't healed. That isn't to say that Mum doesn't get upset, but I think she's moved on and I find it easier to talk to her. In counselling I got in touch with some of my memories, memories I had never really understood. I always thought they were things that had happened in dreams. I remember very clearly standing up in my cot, holding on to Mum, who had this big belly. She was crying and the tears were falling on my head like rain. I used to wonder about that. It seemed so bizarre. This fat Mum and this rain on my head.

'During my counselling it came out that when I didn't have explanations for what had happened to Rosamund I made them up. Dad was very distant after Rosamund died. I presume now that he was trying to hold himself together to go to work, but as a child I thought he was angry. I had this image of him as a kind of god figure and I think a lot of my childhood was quite coloured by this idea that Dad was extremely powerful and had taken Rosamund away and that he could take you away if you didn't play by the rules. I think I felt quite insecure about that and I definitely wanted his approval in a very unhealthy way. I know if some of those old feelings were causing me trouble and I asked him to come with me to a counsellor he would.

'When I went to university he did talk to me about Rosamund, in terms of his dream being completely shattered. Having these lovely little girls. Then Rosamund dying. And missing her. He found it difficult when I was at university, it made him wonder where she would have been. It's all your hopes down the drain. It makes you afraid that your other children are going to die. He talked about that. He felt he had distanced himself from us. So not only had Rosamund died, he'd died too in a way. He'd backed off. I sometimes get a very strong sense of me pursuing him for some kind of reassurance that it's all right. He said a while ago that my daughter reminded him of Rosamund. It was a very poignant moment and I felt very affectionate towards him.

'Losing Rosamund definitely affected my relationships with my other sisters. It came up in the counselling. I didn't want Charlotte, I wanted Rosamund. It felt like a swap. I resented her for a very long time. She knows that. We've talked about it. We lived in the same house just before I got married and we came together in a way that we had never done before and I think we sorted it out then. I think my reaction to Rosamund's death prevented me from really loving Charlotte in a whole-hearted way when we were younger. Now I have a good, loving relationship with all of my younger sisters and I feel OK about being the eldest. But I can remember having a lot of anxiety about the others when we were children. Something was going to happen to them and it would be my fault. I remember thinking that I had to be good. By the time Katy came along I think I was more relaxed. My relationship with her has always been easier. She would have liked to have had a younger sister, so we used to play this game where I was the baby and she was the big sister. It seemed to satisfy something in both of us and used to feel quite healing. I didn't really notice it until about four years ago, but I do pick big sister substitutes as friends. I've always had an older woman as a close friend. I think the main thing about Rosamund dying was that it shattered the feeling of being secure and protected. It's had to be rebuilt.

'There has been one good effect, though, in my relationship with my own daughter. I'm aware that, even though she can't always express it, everything that is happening is going in on some level, that she is a receptor for outside influences. I'm not saying other people are insensitive, but I think I'm extra aware.'

The image of a child's death casting a long shadow over the lives of the remaining family members is one that recurred many times during the accounts of those bereaved of a sibling. Charlotte, now twenty-eight and born only a few weeks after her sister died, believes that Rosamund's death had a huge effect on the family as a whole. She was not terribly keen to express her views at any length, but wanted to contribute something and chose to make it comparatively brief.

'Yes, I think that Rosamund's death was a landmark in the life of the family and impacted profoundly on us all. My own responses, that is, the significance that I gave to the event and the family dynamics that I later experienced, have played a huge part in influencing the choices that I have made in my own life. It is still, if you like, an "active file" around which I have issues unresolved and questions unanswered, and it is probably not an exaggeration to say that, nearly thirty years on, I feel I am still recovering from the shock.

'That said, I am, none the less, wary of giving the event too much significance in terms of being a "cause" of who I am, the way my life is or has been, or, similarly, the way the family is or has been. Rosamund's death was an event that happened; none of us – parents included – were equipped to deal with it at the time and it remained unintegrated. This was reflected, I think, in a certain disintegration of personality in us, the children.

'However, now, as adults, I do feel we are individually addressing and healing this and, for myself, I am confident that I will at some point be able to close this rather long episode and leave whatever pain and confusion there is in the past where it belongs. That's all I want to say.'

The main feeling which Emma recalled about the subject of her dead sister was confusion about who she was. Physically, the two girls were very alike as toddlers, and Emma, now twenty-six, remembered seeing photographs of Rosamund which puzzled her. 'In the course of looking through some family photographs I must have seen pictures of Rosamund with Mum and Dad and I didn't know who she was. I think at some point I thought they were of me or that I was her. They looked similar to some of the photographs of me. I remember it being explained to me, when I was about seven. It was a very hot evening and I remember being very upset. The baby-sitter was there and my sisters asked me what was wrong, but I didn't really say anything. I don't know whether part of it was being a melodramatic little girl, wanting it all to be tragic, or whether I actually was upset. But I think I did feel quite upset about it. I remember feeling very upset for Mum and feeling very bad for her really. Mum had a locket with some of Rosamund's hair in it and at some point I actually cut off some of my hair and put it in a plastic bag in my drawer, almost as if I was trying to copy that, or in case I died. It was almost like a comparison of our hair. Hers was supposed to have been a similar colour to mine.

'I don't think Mum told me about how Rosamund actually died until I was quite a lot older and probably could cope with the details of it, but I remember feeling that it was quite harrowing. I've never really talked to Dad about it. I've talked to Charlotte and Katy in terms of how it feels to have a sister that we didn't know. It's always felt like a bit of a lie to say she was my sister, because it doesn't feel as if she was at all. Lucy's told me a lot about how she felt to have Rosamund die. It's obviously been a really big issue for her. For me, I think there's a sense of feeling a bit left out of it all, although obviously I wouldn't have wanted to be included in all the grief and pain.

'With Lucy I had a feeling that somehow life with the three of us would never be quite as good as the golden days of Rosamund. I used to feel a bit jealous of that. She was this golden girl that we could never be. We were just these pesky little sisters who came along afterwards and would never be as perfect. I don't think my parents put Rosamund on a pedestal, but in all the photographs she looks very sweet and angelic. I remember Mum saying she was bad sometimes and did do naughty things, but with a child of three-and-a-half you don't really get the seriously hefty emotional problems that you might with a teenager. There wasn't really time for her to have caused the sorts of trials and traumas that the rest of us have.

'I think the subject of Rosamund may be a bit taboo with Dad. I'd really like to talk to him about her, but I never have, and when he talks about her his voice drops a bit. I feel that it's not something he really wants to talk about much. I think it would be quite helpful if I could, because I think it affected the way he was with us. When I was small, he seemed very distant. I'm sure Rosamund's death must have had an effect on how he feels about us and how he was as a parent. It seems to have been easier for him to be more involved the older I've got. Perhaps there was some subconscious feeling of not wanting to get too involved when we were younger because of the risk of losing us.'

Emma is training to be an acupuncturist and Chinese herbalist. She believes that her choice of career was considerably influenced by what she perceived as her mother's over-reaction to any illness in the family as she was growing up. 'During my practitioner training we were exploring our feelings about our own health, our own family background of health and how our health was dealt with as children. Looking back, I realized that Mum was quite frightened of us being ill and it seemed that it didn't take much for her to get the doctor out or take us to the surgery. I always thought that was normal, until I discussed it with other people on my course and discovered that it wasn't like that for everybody. Mum's nervousness about us being ill is quite understandable after what happened to Rosamund. But I think it informed my view of health and my own feelings about being ill. During the first few years into my training I realized how much fear I had of illness. This has changed the more I've looked at it, but certainly for a while I was a complete hypochondriac about every single thing that I was studying.

'I also realized that perhaps one of the root causes of my wanting to work with ill people was to do with my own fears of illness and wanting to try and control something which I actually have no control over in myself. Well, it's not that I haven't any control over my own health, because obviously I have in the sense of how I live, what I eat, how I exercise, look after myself and all the rest of it, but, ultimately, I haven't any control over death. I'm going to die. I don't think it's a very big leap from being a hypochondriac to being afraid of death. I think, for me, the fear of death has always been around, just through things like visiting Rosamund's grave at a very young age, knowing that people die and that they can die very young. Perhaps if you haven't got any experience of people in your family dying when they're young you just assume that you will live until you reach an old age. I think I have been afraid of death. It reached a peak a few months into my course, when I began to feel that even my training wasn't going to help me. My whole life and my course at that point seemed so much about illness, illness, illness all the time. I remember having a fortnight when I felt very panic-stricken, felt that I really was going to die quite soon. It was completely irrational, but I think it was all my fears coming to a head. Then something shifted and I suddenly seemed to feel OK. I mean, obviously, I'm only twenty-six and I don't want to die yet. I hope that I'll live quite long, but I don't feel afraid like I did.

'I think, on quite a deep level, doing my training has been a way of working out a lot of my own fears and confusions. In a way, I think it's quite a strange thing to want to work with ill people. Obviously there are lots of good reasons for it – wanting to care for and look after people, to help them get better, realize their own personal power and feel good within themselves. All of these motives are very positive ones. And at the same time, it seems crucial to me to sort out what else is going on. If I'm going to be working with people with illness I think I need to be clear about my own feelings and to be aware of my own issues about illness. That's still an ongoing process.'

Katy, the youngest daughter, believed for a long time that if Rosamund hadn't died she herself would not have been born. Now twenty-four, she has accepted that she was wanted by both her parents, but still has lingering doubts about whether her birth was a way of filling the space left by her dead sister. 'I used to think that, because she was the eldest and I'm the youngest, that if she'd stayed alive I wouldn't have been born. My Mum's always said that she and my Dad wanted five children, but I've always interpreted that wrongly. I didn't listen to what was said. I heard it as they wanted this number and I assumed that I was the "making up the numbers" child. I was a replacement Rosamund. I know they didn't make me a replacement for her, but I felt somehow that her death had made my space, because they didn't have another one after me to make up the five. I mean, obviously you can't replace a child anyway and they did have five, but I felt, in some weird way, her death allowed my birth. I don't mean I feel unloved or unwanted, but our family would have been very different if Rosamund had stayed alive. Things would have worked out differently. There might not have been enough money for five of us. There might not have been the need to have so many children. Having a large family might be a compensation for losing one of them.

'These feelings weren't heavy. I think when you're quite small you have quite a lot of melodramatic thoughts about being adopted or things like that, little tragic things you make up for yourself. I think children do quite often dramatize their lives in some way. It was that sort of thing. I think it must have had some effect on me. It makes me feel a bit like a tagged-on extra, but maybe youngest children feel like that anyway. It's quite an insecure position being the youngest in the family. But I don't think about it a lot and it's not something I've had to have counselling about.

'I must have known about Rosamund when I was quite young. I don't remember a conscious, blinding flash moment at all, but I must have known about her because there was a very large painting in my parents' bedroom of this little girl, looking sweet and angelic, and I remember as a small child thinking that was Rosamund. It wasn't a picture of her, but I thought it was, so I must have known about her. I don't know if I thought, "That's my sister". I just thought, "That's Rosamund". But I don't remember anyone sitting me down and telling me about it or any of us talking about it as a family. That doesn't mean it didn't happen, but I can't remember it. When I got older I did ask questions about what had happened, but it was never talked about as if it had much to do with me. It was something that had happened before I was born, before three of us were born, before my family became itself. It wasn't as if she was part of my family, she was part of a family that had been before me, somehow.

'I've always had this picture of her as totally perfect. In my picture she's always very pretty, she's smiling, she's happy. If I think about her now she'd definitely be married and have a lovely family. She'd be successful. She wouldn't have any of the angst and problems that normal people have. I think I have this vision of her because she died at three, which is a fairly perfect age. Three-year-olds are gorgeous. They haven't had time to become a more rounded person, with good and bad points. And in all the photographs she's very pretty and angelic-looking. She's always been talked about as gorgeous and lovely. I've never heard anyone say she screamed and shouted or had tantrums. I don't think anyone's ever said anything negative to me about Rosamund. I think I would have liked it if I'd heard a few bad things about her as well as the good things. That might have been helpful, because I do think she was put on a pedestal a little bit. Then she would have been more real. She wasn't very real.

'I've never really talked to anybody outside the family about it or thought about it myself too much. I don't feel I have much to say about her because I didn't know her. I mention her to people sometimes, but I feel rather uncomfortable saying I had a sister who died, because people don't like talking about death and it's embarrassing. And although I've been told many times how she died, I don't remember the details. I've blanked them, I think. I have a photograph of her. It's a really sweet photo and it feels like it's the only thing I can have of her, really. Oh dear, I'm going to cry now. I've never cried about Rosamund before. How weird, saying I don't really think anything about it and then I start crying.'

Katy broke off for a few moments to compose herself. Then she started reflecting on the effect Rosamund's death had had on her family, as she perceived it. 'I think it's had massive implications for everybody. I've thought about it more since I got older. It only dawned on me fairly recently that Lucy, my eldest sister, isn't the eldest of the family at all. I don't know why it took so long for me to realize that. She's in the role she wasn't meant to be in, and that must be really difficult for her. She was obviously really traumatized by it. It's tricky to talk about this, but I feel that Rosamund's death caused a big rift in the family. Dad's always been quite a distant sort of chap, but I imagine that he wasn't quite so detached when

Rosamund was alive. I think my Mum – well, this is what I imagine anyway – moved into the "coping and getting on with everything" mode and my Dad moved into a detached mode. And that was the situation I was born into. My mother was more involved in bringing us up. I never doubted that my father loves us, but he always had an air of not quite being there, which he might have had anyway. But I don't think it was helped by having a small child dying. I think it made his attitude to us more protective and yet less willing to get attached at the same time.

'I've never talked to him about it. I don't think we've ever really talked about it as a family at all. Maybe if we'd all talked about it as a family and my parents had said more explicitly, "Our first child died but it doesn't mean we love any of you any less", it would have helped. I know they obviously think that and feel that, but if they'd actually said it, been more explicit, it would have helped. I think you should be very explicit with children. They don't know things, they have to be told.

'I think the person I feel most sorry for is Lucy, because she lost her big sister. She's had a lot of emotional problems and I think a lot of them can be traced back to Rosamund dying. I think she got the rawest deal. I don't mean she had the worst time in terms of pain. She had the worst time in terms of coping with it. I think somebody should have taken more care over what was happening to Lucy, not just my parents, but their relations and friends. I think the way she was affected had many implications and ripples through the family and many effects on the rest of us. I think we all pussyfoot round Lucy because we know that something awful happened to her. I think I was born into a bit of a mess. It would have been nice if it was all sorted out before I was born. But I don't think anyone's to blame. I don't feel resentful and I definitely don't go round thinking my parents failed me and my family at all. I just feel it's a shame that the resources weren't there for everyone to cope.'

CHAPTER 12
The only child

Many of the fathers mentioned by surviving siblings so far have been somewhat shadowy figures, either emotionally detached from their offspring, physically distanced by divorce or separation from the mother of their children, or, as in the case of Francesca Blythe (Chapter 9), already dead.

However, for one young girl, the deaths of both her sister and brother within four months of each other brought about a situation in which her father became the most dominant influence in her life. Racked with grief over the deaths of two of his three children and fearful for the safety of his remaining daughter, he became possessive and over-protective to such a degree that she was hardly allowed out of his sight.

Eva Kaul, now seventy-eight and a widow, living peacefully in a small hamlet in the Wye valley, was born into a prosperous Jewish family in Berlin. When she was a year old, her sister Lilith was born. Her parents had longed for a son and there was great rejoicing at the birth of Peter nearly seven years later. 'My father nearly went crazy with joy, so did my mother,' she recalled. 'We all adored my father, although I was terrified of him too. He didn't have much time for us in the week when we were small. He worked like mad. He was very successful and he loved working. But on Sunday mornings we always could come into his bed and he used to read us fairy stories. He had a gift to entertain children. There we were, my little brother screaming with delight and my mother sleeping through it all. I have some marvellous memories.'

The children had a very protected childhood, with doting parents and financial security. Their parents employed domestic staff and, as well as the apartment in Berlin, they also had a place in the country. Eva and Lilith, with only a year between them, were very close. 'I was very attached to my sister. We were always together. She was extremely charming and good-looking, a very pretty child. She had a radiant smile and everybody adored her. She could charm the birds off the trees. I was quite different. My brother was a very bright child and very good-looking. But he was difficult. He had fits of bad temper and threw himself on the floor sometimes, but my mother was very good. She understood somehow and coped with it. She was marvellous with babies. But she was very bad at getting up in the morning, so my father used to get up and change nappies and feed us. He was a very loving man.'

One fateful Sunday in October 1926, two days before Eva's tenth birthday, all three children were sent out to get some fresh air before lunch. 'A lot of children played on the street and it was our whole desire to play there, but of course we weren't allowed to. To play with a ball in the street was the one thing that was absolutely forbidden. It was a very quiet street, I mean, a car passed there every three hours. Now, we had a very nice girl looking after us and she said if we were good girls she'd give us a ball. She bribed us. So we had the ball. And we went down into the street for a little while. My parents were still dressing for Sunday lunch.

'Nobody ever knew what really happened, but Lilith fell into the road in front of a car and was killed immediately. I don't think she ran after the ball, because we were very, very trained, you know. I think she just fell off the kerb. The thing was, my little brother had got loose from the girl and he ran round the corner. She instinctively ran after him because he was so tiny. It happened in that moment, when the girl's back was turned. I saw it, more or less. I still have this impression of Lilith lying in the road. I ran up like mad, four storeys high, to my parents. Just by instinct. And screamed. My parents weren't even dressed.'

Within a very short space of time the flat was full of friends and relations. 'There was absolute panic. It was like an earthquake for the family, especially for my parents. I had never seen an accident before or knew, really, what death was. The girl came up. I saw her. I still remember how she looked. I've never seen anybody look so ashen. I don't know what else happened. The awful thing was that nobody talked to me. I felt completely lost and alone. Then somebody had the grand idea to get my friend over, so that I shouldn't be all alone. This girl was a bit older than I, but of course that wasn't what I needed. What I really wanted was some grown-up to cuddle me and hold me. But they were all in such a state. Nobody thought of that.'

Later that evening Eva's father did talk to her, and she was appalled to see him cry. 'I think I had never seen an adult cry before and to see my father cry was a most terrible shock. I could still paint the scene in my parents' bedroom on that evening. My father telling me she was dead. I think I tried not to cry, because he said I should cry if I wanted to. I said something like I did not want to make things even worse for them, which sounded good and which I thought I should say, but which I must have read somewhere. I don't think I thought of this phrase myself. In a way my childhood ended there and then. And the very naive and childlike image I had of an all-powerful father who would protect us from all harm and all dangers was smashed for ever. I've suffered from insecurity ever since.'

Eva recalled that her parents went ahead with celebrations for her tenth birthday two days after Lilith had died. 'They didn't want me to feel deprived. There wasn't a proper birthday party as we normally had, but there was the usual large trestle table specially used on such occasions, covered with many lovely presents and a birthday cake with candles. I think that was a really extraordinary thing that they managed to do that.'

In the wake of her sister's death, Eva transferred all her love and affection to her little brother, of whom she had previously taken very little notice. She took to sitting by his bed in the evenings. 'And when he wanted water and wanted this and wanted that, all things not allowed before once he was put to bed, everyone gave in to everything.'

Then, barely four months after Lilith's fatal accident, Peter was taken ill. 'He started crying a bit and my mother thought he just had a bit of wind or something and took him into bed with her. Only my parents were so over-anxious after my sister's death she thought she'd better call the family doctor. She told me this later. The doctor came and he was marvellous. He said immediately, "This child is very ill." I don't know how he knew, because there was no temperature or anything. They took him immediately to the first children's hospital we had in Berlin. The man who ran it knew my family and my mother said later they really bent over backwards to save my brother and couldn't. He was dead next day. My mother wanted a post-mortem, which they did. But they were never quite sure. They thought it may have been the pancreas had stopped functioning. It was extremely unusual, even with grown-ups. And with children about one in ten million.

'My parents had stayed at the hospital overnight, but eventually came home, and it was later that day that they called me into their bedroom, just as they had done after my sister's death, and this time it was my mother who told me, "Now Peter is dead as well." It really only struck me the next day because when I went to school the headmistress called me out from class and asked me if it was really true that my little brother had died. When I confirmed it she went quite pale and was obviously deeply shocked. It was that which brought home to me the enormity of what had happened. And then it was really terrible because now I had lost a second close person in a few weeks.'

From that moment, life was never the same again for Eva. Much of what happened between her parents she only pieced together as an adult, but, as a child, she was only aware that nobody seemed to notice her distress. 'I'm sure I seemed to be all right. I had my friends. I went to school. And I was very good at school. But I suffered terribly. I couldn't sleep. My parents' room was next to mine and I always had to have their door open a bit. I had to see the light on. I had to know they were next door. I sleep with the light on even now. I don't want anybody to think I was neglected. I was marvellously looked after. But I wanted extra comfort and talking about it. My father never talked about it. He reacted absolutely differently from my mother. My father wouldn't say their names any more. He wouldn't talk about them, as if they'd never existed. He took away all the photographs in his private office. And my mother was the opposite. She wanted to talk and she really had nobody, because my father had isolated her from most people. He was very possessive. And he stayed in his office and worked like mad.

'Then he started taking me everywhere. I was collected from school by car, which was very unusual in those days, and went straight to his office. He bought me a lectern sort of thing and I did my homework in the office. It was all fine, but my poor mother sat at home all day alone. When I was about twelve he told me that we would have to be very kind to my mother because she was about to commit suicide. Well, that was good for me! Every day when I went out from school I rang immediately to see whether she was still alive. Now I see of course it must have been absolutely dreadful for my mother, because my father just wouldn't talk about it. I mean, he suffered dreadfully, but he wouldn't do anything to comfort her, apparently. Of course they never got over it. I think there was a great sort of estrangement between my parents. They couldn't share the grief, they couldn't at all.

'For me it was a complete breakdown of everything. All the discipline was thrown overboard. Suddenly there were no rules. That's not good for a child. And I was mainly with grown-ups. My father took me, to my mother's disgust and embarrassment, to places in the evenings where girls, children, really shouldn't go. I mean, one place was a cabaret – Berlin was famous for cabaret – and

I really shouldn't have been there. But he couldn't bear to part with me for a minute. He took me everywhere practically. That was altogether awful, that pressure on me. Not that I should achieve, but that I should be all right. And his over-anxiety all the time. I'm sure that did me a lot of harm.'

Eva had always been encouraged to mix with other children from an early age. Soon after her sister died, she and six or eight of her closest schoolfriends formed a group which they called 'Kränzchen' (little wreath), i.e. a private circle of friends who met regularly in each others' houses. With the help of her father and the use of his studio and office, they even produced a little news-sheet with contributions from all of them. These gatherings were for a few hours only each week. For the rest of the time Eva was always with grown-ups.

'We didn't go to our place in the country for years after my sister and brother died. My parents couldn't bear to go there. But later on I took my friends there for weekends. Yes, I was encouraged to have friends, but I was much too much with grown-ups. Intellectually, I was probably able to take part, but I wasn't really ready for all these things. My parents were so anxious and frightened for me. I felt this pressure. Sometimes I just wanted to flee. I was very, very depressed myself, very unhappy. The first years after my sister died I cried nearly every night. But then during the day I wanted to get away from it. And I couldn't because there was this atmosphere at home. I think my parents were too engrossed in their own grief to be able to think of anything else. I don't blame them for anything. I quite understand that it was dreadful for them. I don't blame myself for what happened to my mother, because I didn't understand at the time. I didn't take much notice of my mother till much later. But my father should have done. He shouldn't have left her like that. It wasn't right.

'My mother was marvellous with babies, but she never had a lot of time to devote herself to us because my father was very demanding, and if the household wasn't absolutely perfect there was hell to pay. She told me later she had always wanted to have a few days just with my brother. And she never had. My heart really broke when she told me that. She wanted more children afterwards, she told me. And I badly wanted another brother or sister. There was no problem financially and they were still young enough then. But my father didn't want any more. He said he couldn't bear something going wrong again. His life was really shattered.

'I was mad about my father for a long time. I adored him and he had a terrific influence on me, to the good and also perhaps to the bad. Then when I got a bit older – but also, again, too young – my mother started to tell me things about him. I was deeply upset by what I was told and and I suddenly turned completely against my father and on to my mother. We had terrible times. He didn't speak to me for a long time, things like that. Now I regret it. Too late, of course. He died. Nowadays I understand a bit more, but at that time I was furious with him. I didn't know what to do. I just couldn't bear it at home. Twice I tried to take a job, but of course my father somehow persuaded me to remain at home.

'My father was not as good as he should have been, but I think life would have been a bit more normal perhaps if my sister and brother had not died. He was a very complex personality. He was a very loving father, yet he was an awful tyrant, a dictator. Family was very strong with him, but there were other women, lots of other women, all sorts, outrageous other women. My mother was very naive. She wasn't ever able to cope with it all. When I got older, one of my boy-friends had a flirt with one of my girl-friends in whom my father had become very interested. She was a very good looking girl. So my father became jealous of this particular boy-friend. Terrible. On the other hand, I owe him such a lot. It's a very mixed thing. He opened the world for me, especially after my sister died. He took me to museums and concerts and cabarets and films. He did a lot for me, good and bad.'

Eva's father died when she was still in her late teens. By then she was very close to her mother. They talked a lot about the deaths of Lilith and Peter, and Eva learned more about the problems in her parents' relationship. Her mother had hundreds of photographs of the two dead children, but, sadly, few of these survived. When Hitler rose to power in Germany, Eva's family decided to move to Holland, where one of her uncles had a factory. Eva, then twenty-three, had been involved in what she called 'a dangerous love affair', and her family decided they wanted to get her away 'as soon and as far as possible'. After a short interval in Holland, Eva was sent to England when family friends had made arrangements for the necessary documents.

'I was forced by the Dutch authorities to come here, as they had so many refugees who had no entry to other countries. This saved my life. I stayed first with these family friends and then started to work as a housemaid, as did most other refugees.' After her arrival in England, just before the start of the Second World War, she went to visit an aunt who was living in Paris and from there went to

Holland, where she saw her mother for the last time. The aunt who lived in France survived the war, but Eva's mother and her mother's sister were both killed by the Nazis. In England Eva met the man who was to become her husband, a fellow German, and after the war they were married.

'It was during the war, by which time I had become a waitress, that I had to undergo psychiatric treatment. I was in a bad nervous state. It was terrible. If somebody said "Good morning" I started crying. The psychiatrist told me he thought I had never worked through the trauma of losing my sister and brother. But my sister's death was just the starting-point. The main problems were very private and very personal. A lot to do with my father. Because I found it difficult to cut loose from him. I had a long treatment for a very bad anxiety state and it was very successful. After the war, when I had somewhat recovered, I started to get back into office work, at first as a copy-typist. Then followed better and better jobs by which time I was back to normal – as normal as I will ever be. My final job with the Medical Research Council was the last step up a fairly long ladder. My poor husband was very patient. The feelings of insecurity I've had to learn to live with. If somebody isn't there when they should be at a certain time I get very panicky. Fortunately, my husband was a very sympathetic man. He understood, and when he was going to be late he used to ring me.'

Eva never had children of her own. 'I would have been over-anxious, I think. Because of the scars I have, the insecurity, because from one minute to the next my whole world was shattered, I felt I would never trust life any more. The thing that remains is that when something is wrong with my cat I get quite hysterical. I can't control it. I start shaking. I feel sick. My fears now are all concentrated on the cat.'

CHAPTER 13
Happy families

As we have noticed from the case histories already dealt with, the death of a child brings about significant changes to the family structure. Every child has his or her own sense of what a family should be, based initially on personal experience of his or her own family. Later, that perception of family may change as the child comes across different types of families, either through reading about them, watching television or noticing what kinds of families schoolfriends appear to have. Very few people grow up without ever having compared their own relations unfavourably with some idealized fantasy of the perfect family. Most eventually come to terms with the reality of their situation and accept their family for what it is.

For those bereaved of a sibling in childhood, however, the fantasy takes a different turn. Francesca Blythe (Chapter 9) fuelled her fantasies of a 'normal' family by voraciously reading book after book about family life. My daughter Lucy (Chapter 11) resented the loss of her 'first' family and found it hard to adjust to the new set-up with three more sisters born in fairly quick succession. Eva Kaul (Chapter 12) longed for her parents to have another baby when she became the only child after the death of her sister and brother. For these bereaved children and, indeed, for many who lost a sibling, the change in the family structure was a bitter pill to swallow.

For Ann Howard, who lost her baby sister when she was five years old, there was a powerful yearning to be part of a large family. Her parents did have another daughter when Ann was seven, but she always felt troubled by the big gap in their ages. 'I loved the idea of families,' she told me. 'I loved to read books where there were large families. I always envied families on beaches where there seemed to be a lot of children. Once my parents brought the daughter of some friends on holiday with us. She was older than my little sister and I really loved it that there were three of us. I really wanted to have children of my own and when I married after leaving university I started a family straight away. I had three children quite close together.'

The death of her sister also prompted strong feelings of wanting to make reparation. She was more aware of her parents' distress than her own, both at the time of the death and for many years afterwards. Her concern to 'make things right' for people led her into a career as a social worker. Her present job is in a hospice for the terminally ill. It is only in the last few years, having been on a counselling course and also having received some individual counselling, that she has begun to look at the background to her pattern of behaviour as a 'rescuer'.

Ann was born during the Second World War, when her father was away on active service. She was three by the time he returned. During those early years she formed a very strong bond with her mother. It was this close relationship, she told me, which 'saved' her when the family suffered the loss of the second child, because she felt so secure in her mother's affections. There was never any question of her feeling that she should have died instead of her baby sister. Any guilt she later felt was to do with her feeling powerless to make things right for her grieving parents, particularly her mother.

She recalled her father's return as something of a shock. Nevertheless, she adjusted fairly well to having him back in the family, to the arrival of her baby sister Jean when she was four and to a subsequent move from their flat in London to a house in Birmingham. Ann showed me a photograph of herself with Jean, taken when the baby was about seven months old. In it she looks like the archetypal loving older sister, but when I asked her if she could remember Jean at all she said she couldn't. 'I can remember my mother bathing her. That's about all. And I know I was upset when she died. But I think it was more to do with my parents being upset.'

Jean died at the age of fifteen months after contracting meningitis and being taken into the local children's hospital. Ann was told that her sister was ill, but was never taken to see her in hospital. 'I remember crying at night and being worried that Jean was going to die. And my mother saying, "No, it's going to be all right." I think in those days parents weren't encouraged to stay with their children in hospital. My parents didn't have a phone and my father used to go out every morning to ring the hospital to see how she was. I remember him coming back one morning to say that my sister had died. We were all in the kitchen. I remember my mother was doing my hair, because I had plaits, and her first words were, "Oh, how terrible for you that you had to walk back, knowing that." She was trying to comfort him, I think. Then, really, it's a blur, although I do remember some people coming to the door and bringing a wreath from the people in the street. And my mother got upset, although she thought it was a nice gesture because we hadn't lived there very long.'

On the day of the funeral Ann went to school as usual, and was taken to have lunch with a neighbour. Her clearest memory of that day was of being given poached egg on toast for lunch! 'After that, my strongest memories are of my parents being upset. I always felt aware of my mother being sensitive to things. If meningitis was ever mentioned she would give a gasp and maybe start to cry. And Jean's birthday was 21 April, the Queen's birthday, which was unfortunate in terms of anniversaries because it was always a reminder to my mother. Then there was this picture of me and Jean. It used to be in my parents' bedroom. It was a symbol of sadness. It didn't seem to involve me. It was very much this baby that had gone. I didn't feel sad myself, but I felt that my parents did. And that made me uncomfortable. But I think my parents did the best they could. They did actually tell me what had happened to Jean. There wasn't any tale that she'd just gone to sleep or gone to be with Jesus. I think I understood it was final. I feel sad now that my mother didn't have any sort of counselling. It wasn't available in those days. She tended to be an anxious person and used to get depressed.'

However, Ann said she never sensed any change in her parents' feelings towards her after Jean died. Nor did she recall any particular problems at school. 'I can't remember, but I'm sure I must have been jealous of Jean. I tended to be naughty and have tantrums and shout and scream. I think I was quite an aggressive child. Maybe that was a reaction to what had happened, I don't know. I was forever coming home with a nosebleed from being knocked and punched. But I think, on the whole, my childhood was quite happy. My parents didn't put any restraints on me. I was allowed to roam around quite a bit on my bike, which you could in those days. So, no, I don't think they altered towards me because of Jean. But I changed. There was this whole sense of protecting them.'

How did she feel when the new baby came along? 'I loved it. I was really keen because I suppose I was quite lonely in lots of ways. I was nearly seven and at that age I think you're over the jealousy thing. She came on Christmas Day and it was terribly exciting because she was one of the Christmas babies with her photograph in the *Birmingham Mail*. One positive thing that had happened after Jean's death was that the neighbours whose phone my father had used became really good friends. We always used to spend Christmas with them. When Liz was born my father went to the hospital and I had Christmas with these friends. It was lovely for my mother to have another baby, although she was forty-two then and she had high blood pressure and suffered quite a bit.'

Ann sensed that things improved a little between her parents after the arrival of Liz. Jean was still talked about sometimes, although Ann herself never brought up the subject or asked any questions about her. 'I felt I didn't want to upset them. I think I repressed some things. My mother got very depressed when I left home and I felt guilty about that. I also felt guilty about not living how they perhaps wanted me to live, changing my politics, things like that. I think perhaps I disappointed them academically, too. My father wanted me to be a doctor and I did rebel at that. I didn't want to spend six or seven years studying.

'I think I got more in tune with the whole thing when I had my own children, in terms of understanding my mother more. She started talking more about Jean. And she told me – and this is the terrible thing – that she had a sister who died. There was a brother, my mother and then this baby who picked up a cold from her. There had definitely been some blame put on her for bringing the cold home. And then to have her own baby die. It must have been awful for her. I think it made a difference to how she treated me after Jean died. I never felt any sense of blame. When my mother died and we had to go through her things there was this purse, and inside it she'd got a picture of herself holding me as a baby. That really touched me.'

She was less close to her father, probably because of his absence during the first three years of her life. 'He was a very outgoing person. He used to laugh and joke a lot. I think he used to hide his feelings a great deal. My mother told me he was devastated because he'd missed my early childhood. Then my sister was born and she died. He was devoted to my mother and when she died he had her ashes scattered over Jean's grave, so obviously there was something still there for him. I wish now I'd talked to him more about Jean before he died. He was closer to my sister Liz. Here was a child he was fully involved with from the start. I don't think Liz ever felt there were high expectations of her as a replacement for Jean, although in a sense that's what she was. She told me she used to think it was quite exciting that she'd got this dead sister whom she hadn't known, because it meant she had an interesting past to tell people.

'I've got this elderly uncle I can talk to about the past. I really love that. He went to Jean's funeral and he implied that it was very harrowing. I think that's why parents don't want children to go. They know they might break down and they don't want their children to see them in that state. They want to shield them. I understand that, but I have felt cheated of the funeral. Years later I went to a child's funeral. It really brought it home to me. She was the daughter of a friend of mine, killed in a car accident. She was a bit older than Jean and there was a brother who was five. The parents were very much into an open way of doing things. They brought her body back from the undertaker and had her coffin at home. They wanted their son to see her because he might have worried about her being damaged in the accident. They wanted friends to go and see her too. I did, and I almost felt it was a way of coming to terms with Jean dying. The funeral service was very moving. Everyone was very upset, but it did help a lot. It started the healing process.'

Like Ann Howard, Beryl Friend has a strong sense of the importance of family. Her beloved eldest sister, Estella Seaton, died more than sixty years ago, and Beryl has always striven to keep her memory alive. She makes a point of taking flowers to Estella's grave on the anniversary of her death, a journey of some sixty miles from her home in Sussex to the London suburb of Isleworth. Ten years ago she researched, wrote and published a history of her family. It features a photograph of Estella, a beautiful and stylish young woman with the fashionable bobbed haircut of the 1920s.

Several times during her conversation with me, Beryl became very tearful. She wrote to me later: 'I have been trying to solve the mystery of my weeping when I recalled the events of a death which happened over 60 years ago. I think I have detected similar emotions in old soldiers on TV, describing the Battle of the Somme, etc. These are men of 90 years old with tears in their eyes, which I doubt they shed when they were young men seeing their comrades dying round them. There must be some change in people as they get older. I have never discussed Estella's death in detail with anyone else and I wish I could have been more "matter of fact" when I talked to you.'

Neither Beryl nor her older brother Albert and younger sister Alma had ever talked much with each other about the death of their sister, either at the time or during the following years. 'It's odd, isn't it?' she said. 'When you're children you sort of accept it. You don't say, "How do you feel? Isn't this awful?" But it comes back later. My brother, who's a military historian living in Canada, wrote to me just after the fiftieth anniversary of our sister's death and told me he had been thinking a lot about Stella (as we called her) and the events surrounding her death. And recently my sister, who's a retired nurse, came to stay, and I started to talk to her about it. We've never done that before.'

According to Betty Rathbone, it's never too late to try and sort out the past. Indeed, she felt that for people whose relatives had balked at talking much about traumatic events when they happened, it was always worth going back to the subject, even after a long interval. 'It may be that people hang on to pain for years and years and years. It's a way of coping which has worked for them, even though it may have been very dysfunctional for somebody else. Sometimes, as life has gone on and better things have happened, they may be willing to drop their defences. I don't think there's such a thing as being too late, as long as memory is still there.'

The memories are certainly still there for Beryl. Stella was her mother's first child; the second was a boy who died of meningitis at the age of three. Then came a gap of several years before Albert, Beryl and Alma were born within three-and-a-half years of each other. 'Stella was the provider of treats. I don't know how she put up with us. We used to have arguments about whose turn it was to go out with Stella on a Sunday. We lived near the Thames at Richmond and she would take us on the river. When my mother took us to the cinema it was in the stalls, but if Stella took us it was the best seats in the circle. There was often open warfare between my parents, and Stella was the peacemaker, so that when there was a row brewing she'd take us out of it. And she would smooth things out between my parents by making a joke of it. She also played the piano and we used to have musical evenings, with my mother singing. When she went out, for instance on a Saturday night, we'd watch her dress up and smell her scent. In the morning we'd wake up and she would have left us chocolates on the dressing table.'

Those happy days came to an abrupt end just before Christmas 1932, when Stella was twenty-one and Beryl was ten. Stella woke feeling unwell and their mother insisted that she should stay in bed, despite Stella's protests that she must go to work at her job as a GPO telegraphist in London. The next morning she was desperately ill with septicaemia caused by an infected spot on her face. She was rushed into hospital and died a few days later. She was buried on Christmas Eve. Beryl remembered her father telling her that Stella was dead. She was about to go to school, where they were having a Christmas party. Her father wrote a note for her to give to her teacher. 'Really, when I think about it I should have been sent home. I just sort of sat there. Nobody at school said anything to me about it. Alma was at home because she was in bed with flu, and Albert's school had already broken up.' Her mother, Beryl thought, had taken to her bed.

'The undertakers brought Stella's body to the house. They used to in those days. I remember I saw her in the coffin. I didn't ask to, but I was taken in with my brother. I didn't go to the funeral. I stayed at home to look after Alma and prepare for the people who came back from the funeral. But my brother went. A lot of people came back to the house. There were lots of young women from her office and her young man, as we called him. It seemed like a big crowd to me. After that my mother went into a state of misery. We just accepted it. Understandable.'

Beryl's mother never discussed with them the effect Stella's death might have had on the three surviving children. 'She used to talk to other people. She would recount the story of Stella's death to new friends or new relations. And she would cry. But nobody asked us how we felt. At the time I didn't think that was odd, and I'm not blaming anyone now. I mean, we weren't crying any more. I can't remember crying any more after the first news that she was dead. I felt my mother was entitled to be the chief mourner. But when I was talking to Alma recently she said she thought our mother was self-absorbed in her own troubles and didn't think much about how we felt. It hadn't occurred to me at the time that she should. Alma also said she believed Stella was Mother's favourite. She said, "I always think Mother didn't help much when she said she'd lost the best one, she'd lost her friend." And I said I thought it was understandable. Stella was her first-born. She had a different relationship with her because Stella was grown-up. They used to go shopping together, buying hats and things like that. As a child, I think I just accepted things as they were. We weren't a terribly affectionate family. There wasn't a lot of kissing and cuddling. So I just sat back and thought, "Obviously, she's upset." I expected her to do the weeping and be miserable. I wasn't supporting or criticizing. I just stood aside.'

So the three remaining Seaton children grew up bereft of their 'provider of treats' and with parents whose rows became much more bitter, without the peacemaker to pour oil on troubled waters. Looking back, Beryl said she was always grateful that all three of them survived into adulthood. 'Our mother was always doom-laden. Well, she did have two children who died. She always dreaded the worst. And I think I'm the complete pessimist. I take the view that if something awful doesn't happen that's a bonus. I think that's probably the main effect on me of Stella's death.'

Beryl never stopped missing Stella and grieving over her death. 'When I was older my mother gave me Stella's watch, which I wore all through the war. Eventually it packed up, but I couldn't throw it away. I've still got it. And one of her handbags, which I've still got. I used that, a leather handbag, during the war. It's very shabby now, but I can't throw it away. It's important to me that she's not forgotten.'

CHAPTER 14
Denial and disbelief

The need to talk about the death of somebody close is very powerful. Bereaved adults, if they can find a willing listener, will go on and on about the dead person, reliving again and again the events surrounding the death. Organizations such as Cruse Bereavement Care and The Compassionate Friends provide just this sort of safe space where the grief-stricken can share their feelings. Children, however, are often denied the opportunity for expressing their conflicting emotions in the wake of a sibling's death. As a result, they may carry with them for years all the unspoken thoughts and feelings which, if they had been able to express them at the time, would have helped them through a healthy mourning process.

Another important part of the business of coming to terms with death is making some sort of sense of the known evidence. Being able to ask 'How?' and 'Why?' and receiving honest answers will help to give the death some reality. For children, this is crucial. Without proper information they are likely to fantasize about what really happened and their imaginary scenarios may cause great unease. Alice McKee (Chapter 5) imagined that her sister wasn't really dead, but had been put away in a home for the mentally handicapped. Dale Thomas (Chapter 8) had gory visions of his brother's head being chopped off.

Of course, some of the questions about death are very difficult to answer. This doesn't mean that some attempt cannot be made. The young enquirer needs answers which help him or her to understand the reality of the situation. John Bowlby, in a section about mourning in his masterly work on the importance of the parental relationship to the mental health of children, puts it this way: 'Only, indeed, when he is given true information, and the sympathy and support to bear it, can a child or adolescent be expected to respond to his loss with any degree of realism.'[1]

Mary P., whose dearly loved older brother Tom died when she was thirteen, was allowed none of the facilities which might have helped her to work through the trauma of his death. Because her parents appeared to close their minds to the whole business, she made up her own version of what had happened and refused to accept that Tom was dead. For about eighteen months she lived in a surreal world, believing that her parents were crazy and that she was the only person who was in touch with reality. 'I was probably certifiable for most of that time,' she told me.

Now fifty-six, with two grown-up children and married to her second husband, Mary works as a teacher in the Midlands. A thoughtful, caring and highly intelligent woman, she came to terms with the anguish of losing the brother she described as her 'boon companion' many years ago. But the nightmare of the years after his death is still very vivid in her mind.

The circumstances which created Mary's special bond with her brother, who was nearly three years older than her, were a home in which there were two sick parents who pushed much of the responsibility of running the household onto their children and who were never able to share much in the way of communicating either feelings or information. In other words, there were many secrets in the family. The couple had lost their first child, a son called Tony, before Mary was born, but it was never talked about. 'To this day I don't know when he died or anything about him. My mother never ever discussed him, even when I had my own children.'

Mary was two when the Second World War broke out and her father joined the RAF. 'I was left with my mother, who was a very neurotic, highly strung woman, and my brother Tom. Partly because we didn't have a father around and partly because my mother was convinced she wouldn't last very long, with her bad heart, she consciously made us very close. My brother was given responsibility for me for everything. He was the one who took me down to the air-raid shelter and looked after me. He was the one who took me to start school when I was five. She shied away from emotional situations and was happy to put them onto him. And he protected me from her wrath. We were thrown together on our own resources and we were good friends. We shared a sense of humour and we both liked things that our parents didn't, like classical music, which we used to listen to secretly on the radio. When the war ended and my father came home he was an invalid for the rest of his life. He had long patches in bed. In many ways that intensified my relationship with Tom. We had to take over a lot more of the responsibility of the housework. Later, when we both went to grammar schools, we travelled part of the journey on a bus together into town and out. And we did our homework together.'

The family was always very poor, so Tom left school after taking his O levels. He had a job to go to, but first he was spending the summer doing a holiday job at an Army camp near Middlesbrough, many miles from the family home outside Newcastle. Mary had saved up all year to go to a school camp. It was the first time either of them had been away from home or been apart from each other. Tom went off first and was due home the day before Mary returned from her trip.

'I half hoped he might turn up in town to meet me. But he didn't. So there I was on my way home on the bus out of town and a "good lady of the parish" got on and came and sat next to me. After a bit she said, "I'm terribly sorry to hear . . .", and I said, "To hear what?" And she said, covering her face with her hands, "You don't know? I shouldn't have said anything." And I thought "Somebody has to be dead." It was a toss–up whether it was my father or my mother. She was always having minor heart attacks and he was an invalid. I was desperately shocked, but thought I'd just get home and Tom would be handling the situation.

'I got off the bus and walked down our road and I met my grandmother, who had just left our house. I asked her what had happened and she said there had been an accident. She told me to go home and not talk out in the street. When I went into the house it was all totally surreal. While we'd both been away my mother had taken it into her head that it was a good time to change things round and redecorate. She'd even made alterations to the fireplace. There was nothing in the living room that was recognizable. There was a neighbour who'd never been in the house before. She was somebody my mother didn't have much truck with, but who'd come in to hang up the new curtains.

'So it wasn't the house I'd left, this person being there was very strange and my mother and father were both completely unrecognizable. They'd known about Tom's death since the morning and it had changed their faces. But the most staggering thing was that they were both there. So I knew there had been some error in what I'd been told and I must have looked very shocked. At first, nobody actually said or did anything. Then my mother said, "Has somebody told you?" And I said, "I met this lady on the bus and she said she was very sorry." But still nobody said what had happened. I went off and looked all round the house and after a bit I said, "Where's Tom?" And they looked at me in a very, very shocked way as if to say, "You know what's happened." But they didn't actually say. At that point I didn't want anybody to say. As long as nobody said it, nothing had happened. They were obviously grief-stricken and desperate. I can remember seeing my father's hand on the back of a chair and his knuckles were white. I suppose I knew inside that it could only mean one thing, but I didn't want to hear it and they certainly didn't want to say it. So we sat around and had a cup of tea.

'A bit later on I said something like, "What happened?" I remember quite clearly my mother saying, "He's not coming back, you know." And I was prepared to believe that it meant, literally, he wasn't coming back from the place where he'd been staying. Later I asked my mother if she had seen Tom and if he had come home the day before. She said he had been on his way home when the police came and said there had been an accident.

She and my father had gone to the hospital in Middlesbrough, but they hadn't actually seen Tom. I thought, "Obviously there's been some stupid mistake." Much later on I opened a drawer for something and there was this green fountain pen that had been my brother's pride and joy. My father took it out and said, "He would have wanted you to have this." I remember clearly that this was a sort of watershed, because I thought that anybody who could say that my brother would have wanted me to have his pen, which he wouldn't let me breathe on, never mind touch, would believe anything. "Boy," I thought, "wait till Tom comes back and I tell him. What a laugh we'll have." '

The next day when Mary got up, there was a neighbour in the house doing the washing up. She was told that her mother had gone to the inquest, which she assumed was something like a post-mortem. She confidently expected her mother to come back having realized her mistake about Tom. When her mother returned, Mary asked her again if she had seen her brother and was told, 'No, of course not.' That evening one of her brother's friends called round and her parents gave him Tom's bike, saying this was what Tom would have wanted. Again, Mary reacted with disbelief and amazement. She shouted at her parents and was told she must realize that Tom wasn't coming back. But still nobody said the word 'Dead'.

Mary can recall nothing of what happened over the next couple of days. 'I remember sort of becoming aware that it was Sunday afternoon. There was my Aunt Millie and another aunt and uncle who'd come up from London. And the house had mysteriously sprouted flowers. The bathroom was full of them, they were laid down the stairs, they were everywhere. And still there was this surreal room where everything had changed. My mother and father were altered people, relatives from London were living in the house. Everywhere was full of flowers. I began to think I had died and was just a ghost, not communicating with people. They couldn't see me. Because nobody spoke to me, I thought that perhaps I was invisible. It all sounds mad, doesn't it?

'The next day, about mid-morning, my mother was looking out of the window and she suddenly fell to her knees and began to pray in a very distressed way. And there was this perfectly ordinary black van, not a hearse, driving slowly into the corner of our street. There were quite a lot of our neighbours at their doors and windows watching this. It drew up outside where we lived and as I watched, fascinated, these men pulled out a coffin and started to carry it into our house. I was still, manically and euphorically, certain that everybody had gone mad except me. There was a lot of clattering downstairs in the living room – I realize now they'd moved the sofa and put up some trestles – and then we all came downstairs while they opened the coffin. I watched them take out these long screws and I absolutely *knew*, not thought, I *knew* that when they got the lid off that coffin they'd see their mistake. I knew it wasn't possible, I knew nobody had seen him. I knew nobody had said the word "Dead". My mother stepped forward and looked into the coffin and she gave a kind of strangled gasp, the response of a mother who's seen her son dead for the first time. I misinterpreted it as shock at her mistake. So then I stepped forward, feeling triumphant, and peered in.

'And what was so shocking was not just that it was my brother, but the fact that his was the only unravaged face I'd seen since I got home. He was the only thing that hadn't changed. He was just paler, but he was himself. He had a reality that nobody else had. People trailed in and out all day bringing flowers and looking at Tom and saying, "Doesn't he look natural?" Eventually we all went to bed and I got up again, very late in the night when everybody was asleep, and went downstairs and sat on a chair beside the coffin and talked to Tom. I told him everything that had happened since I'd got home, what they'd said and how they were all behaving. I mentioned his bike and his pen, everything.'

Mary was bought a new school coat to wear at the funeral and given some flowers to carry. She recalled feeling detached from the service and the interment. 'I wasn't upset. I just thought it felt ludicrous, some stupid ritual they were going through, when it hadn't really happened. We went back to the house and had tea and sandwiches and people talked about other people who'd died. As though my brother had died. It was impossible. It was unacceptable. And the next morning everybody went on as though everything was normal, as though you could do that if somebody had died. I thought they were all stark raving crazy. Looking back now, I realize who was the mad one.

'Then the post came, with my brother's O level results, and everybody cried. When everybody had lost interest I put his results in the saddle-bag of my bike and pedalled round to the churchyard. These memories are very strong. All the flowers were heaped up and I made a little sort of hole in the flowers to the earth and shouted down "French, Grade B". And so on. I was probably certifiable. As the partner who was holding the fort until he was better, until he was back, until it was all right, I looked after his results paper. I kept all his things that I knew he wouldn't want to get rid of safely in a drawer. I memorized important things that happened, I made mental notes of the things that people were doing and saying and I guarded it all up, so that on his return it would be all right. And all that really happened was that time went on and nothing happened. And it wasn't talked about. If I mentioned my brother my father said, "Shush. Don't upset your mother." Tom's things came back from the hospital, including the money he had earned, soaked in blood. My father burned the money. And he burned Tom's shoes when my mother wasn't there. And nobody talked about him. Nobody permitted any kind of grief. I went out and about in the village after a few days and I felt like a ghost. I was ignored. All our mates crossed the street. I felt like I'd done something terrible.

'When I went back to school in September nobody said anything. Presumably, the nice nuns at the convent were being discreet and had told everybody not to talk about it. His birthday came in November, but we didn't mention it in case it upset somebody. Then winter came and I used to call in at the churchyard on the way off the bus from school. I'd clear away any ice or snow off the grave, because it was cold, and talk to Tom and talk to him and talk to him. Occasionally I thought I saw him in a crowd or passing by on a bike in the street. But when I caught the person up it wasn't Tom. And eventually, I think about eighteen months later, I actually realized what "dead" means. They made him cease to exist. Oh God, I still find it so emotional. They left me charged with the responsibility of being the only person who believed that Tom had lived. They erased him by not talking. We didn't talk about anything he'd liked.

We didn't do anything that he'd liked doing. We didn't listen to any radio programmes that he'd enjoyed because that might remind people. For years I went on believing that I had to be the witness to his having lived. I felt amputated, like somebody who's had a leg removed, but nobody will ever believe you once had two.'

There was never any break in the family silence about Tom all the time that Mary was growing up. At age twenty she married and left home. On her wedding day she wanted to leave her bridal bouquet on Tom's grave, and told her mother she planned to go to the churchyard after the reception on her way home to get changed. 'And she said, "You can't make an exhibition of yourself like that. You don't want to remind people and embarrass them like that. But, if you wish, when you've gone away and it's all over, I'll take the flowers round myself in the evening and put them on the grave." I had wanted to go to the graveyard in my wedding dress. But I always did what my mother said. When we came back a week later from our honeymoon and those bridal flowers were still in her house I could have killed her.

'Her way of dealing with Tom's death was to keep her head up. It was as if he had done something embarrassing. On the morning of the funeral I heard her say to somebody, "I will not cry. I will not let anybody see that my son has brought grief to my household." She was very proud of her family and her household and she always believed that other people were waiting for her downfall. She wouldn't express her grief because she thought people would relish her misfortune. And, because she felt like that, she expected it of me. The rule was, "We do not make a fuss in public and we don't cry at home either." As an adult, I have heard my mother say, "We lost the boy." I have never heard her say, "He's dead. He died. He was killed in an accident." My father never spoke about it because he didn't dare. She was the dominant one. When my father died my mother and I had a slight contretemps – she was ill at the time – about the announcement in the local paper. I wanted her to put "father of Tom (deceased)" and she said "No. Definitely not." But when she died I put Tom's name in her announcement. We never had a gravestone for Tom because we couldn't afford it. So when my mother died about two years after my father – they're buried in a different churchyard from Tom – I had a gravestone made with a joint inscription for them and on the bottom I had it inscribed "And their beloved son Tom." Even though he's not buried there, he's remembered.

'Years later I went north for some reason or other with my son, who was married by then. We went together to the churchyard where Tom was buried. It's closed now and all overgrown and my son said, "How can you know the place?" But I knew. We put a little African violet there amongst the grass and I said to my son, "I'm going to let it go." But the strongest feeling I had even then, more than twenty years on, was that I wanted to dig down and find a bone – a finger bone was what I thought in my mind – to have and keep as proof. I wanted something to say, "Tom really lived. He really died." But I recovered from that.'

There was a long silence after Mary had finished talking. Then she made a sound which might have been laughter or tears, or perhaps a mixture of both, and said, 'That's the first time I've told that story from beginning to end to anybody.'

There was no need for me to ask what Mary would have preferred to have happened in the wake of Tom's death, but she added it anyway. 'I think for a start they could have sent somebody to meet me. It's not the sort of thing you want to hear on a bus from a stranger. If they had told me the truth from the first moment, I'd have been grief-stricken, but it would have been real. It wasn't real for years. I think I was mentally unhinged for a very long time. My parents' generation were accustomed to death. People didn't talk about it, but everybody knew about it. They had mechanisms for dealing with it. But I didn't. I couldn't bear their ordinariness when something so vast was happening.'

NOTE

1. John Bowlby, *Attachment and Loss*. The Hogarth Press and the Institute of Psycho-Analysis, 1980.

CHAPTER 15
Breakdown and breakthrough

One of the key factors which discriminates against children after a bereavement is their lack of personal power. For the most part, adults can choose how to conduct themselves. They can cry and cry, talk it through, seek counselling, find comfort in religion or obtain some other outlet for their grief. They can, if they wish, go into a decline and refuse to be comforted. They can take the Stoic's course, putting on a brave face and not allowing themselves to sink under the weight of their grief. In practical matters, too, adults have some say. They can ask to see the dead body, have some input into the funeral arrangements, decide if, indeed, they really want to attend the funeral. They can make decisions about disposing of the dead person's personal effects and have some control over the reshaping of the family in the wake of the loss of one of its members.

Children, on the other hand, are very much at the mercy of parents and other adults in their lives. What they want and what they feel – or are allowed to feel – will be determined by what is considered appropriate by those in charge of them.

Paul Hithersay, one of the few men who offered to share his experiences of losing a sibling, was not a child when the death occurred, but a young man of just twenty-one. However, he was still living at home with his parents, his nineteen-year-old sister and seventeen-year-old brother, so he did get caught up in the family's response to the tragedy. He felt he was able to exercise some personal power in the aftermath of the bereavement. His parents did allow him to make choices; for example, letting him and his sister decide whether or not they wished to go and view the body of their dead brother. Looking back, however, he said he was not very grown-up emotionally at that time and that this had impeded his mourning process.

Paul is now forty and divorced. He works as an art teacher in a large comprehensive school and lives with his teenage son. On the night of his brother's accident, Paul and his girl-friend were with a crowd of young people at a friend's flat. His brother joined them later, but then decided he wanted his guitar. At first he rang home to see if his father would bring it, but when his father said it was too late to turn out, he was offered a lift home by one of the other young men.

'I never liked this bloke for some reason, and I had this strange feeling, not exactly a clearly focused premonition, but just a weird sense of something ominous,' recalled Paul. 'When I saw my brother running downstairs to the front door I just said to him "Mind how you go." About one in the morning my girl-friend and I walked back to my Mum and Dad's house, after we'd received a phone call from my Dad asking if we'd seen my brother. He hadn't turned up. As we were walking along we saw a car, a Morris 1000, all twisted up with the windscreen out, smashed glass everywhere and a lamp-post down. And I just knew, I knew. Just after we got home the police arrived and said my brother was in hospital.'

Paul, his parents and his sister went straight to the hospital. The whole experience seemed unreal. 'I just felt I was lifted out of it into a state of disbelief. I can remember having a strange sensation of stiffness round the back of my head. It was just as if we were watching *Z Cars*, which was one of the top TV programmes at the time. We were watching it and we weren't really in it. And yet we knew it was real.'

Paul's brother had smashed his skull and suffered terrible brain damage. He died a week later. Had he pulled through the accident he would have been severely retarded, and this knowledge helped the family, to some extent, to come to terms with his death. 'He was such a lively bloke and very popular. He was a really accomplished guitar player and a very, very good driver, which was another irony, because if he'd have been driving there wouldn't have been an accident. We knew that if he wasn't going to recover from the injuries we didn't want him to come back home as a cripple and a vegetable. He'd rallied once in the hospital, just long enough, we felt, to know that he was done for. Then he just faded out again. We believed he'd sorted out that he didn't want to come back. So we all had that as something to hang on to. So we talked a lot, but we couldn't really believe what had happened. How we all got round it was anger. It sort of galvanized us. We were all of us really, really angry.

'There was a big funeral. All his schoolfriends turned up. It was a cold, wet day in July. I can still remember this feeling of detachment watching the coffin go off, with, on top, this expensive electric guitar he'd bought by working at weekends. I was more concerned with my parents and my sister and I detached myself from my own emotions. I felt this responsibility to keep it all together. I didn't want to crack up and upset everybody else. We all tried to get on with our lives, but for a long time we felt he would walk in any minute. We just couldn't get used to his loss. My Mum and Dad decided to burn all his exercise books in the garden one evening. It was a kind of rite. And we knew it was. And it was terrible. Then his A Level results came through and they were all Grade A. He'd struggled at school and felt inferior because he was at a secondary school, whereas my sister went to a grammar school and I went to a technical college. And those results were brilliant. I suppose we gradually accommodated his loss into our lives, although I don't think my Dad, who's dead now, ever sorted it out. He was angry for a long time. One of the feelings I had very strongly when my brother died was that I wished it could have been me. Not out of guilt, but because I felt he was worth more than me. I said that to my Dad once and he was furious.'

Paul had never let himself cry over his brother's death. He had wept a little in bed at night while his brother was in hospital, but once the death was announced he put a block on all his feelings of grief and concerned himself with looking after the rest of the family. He completed his college course, married, and had children, but after seven years he and his wife parted. 'I still hadn't let myself get in touch with my emotions. So when we split up it was fine, because nothing was going right with us. I wanted her to be happy and I knew I was making her miserable. I wasn't upset by it. I felt quite freed from a failure I'd made. But then I fell madly in love with this really strange woman who didn't seem real somehow. The relationship suddenly ended and it was like a bereavement. And I actually began to feel true emotions. I went really down. And when I was in that state I walked into the kitchen one morning and suddenly everything about my brother's death crowded in. I collapsed in tears.

'When I was experiencing the joyful side of the relationship with this woman I was actually allowing somebody to get right through my defences. I just let myself be completely open. I hadn't realized until then what being vulnerable meant, because I'd always had these strong barriers that helped me to cope with my brother dying – or I thought they had helped me to cope. I'd been detached about my wife taking two of my children off to France. I'd always had this disconnection between feeling and intellect. It was self-protection. But when this relationship ended so abruptly I was open and vulnerable. And suddenly I had all this pain and confusion and disappointment to deal with. And all the grief for my brother came up. It went on for about two months. I cried a lot, but I recognized that some of my tears were for me, for my loss, not for him. I wrote lots of poetry during that time and did lots of drawings and paintings. But it was a really mad struggle. I was working at the time and I found that difficult. But I had a lot of support from other people, who actually started making me laugh again. That was the best medicine.'

One of the main consequences of losing his brother is what Paul describes as 'a background fear'. He has fears for the safety of his son, who is now the same age as his brother was when he died. 'I can get really crippled with worry. And I do think it's difficult for me to form deep emotional relationships because I'm afraid of losing the person. So the barriers come up again. I think what frightens me is loss of control. The powerlessness I feel is lack of control over reality.'[1]

Feelings of powerlessness and lack of control haunted Beth Jordan for nearly two decades after her sister died. As the only child left in the family, she could find no outlet for her own feelings over the death of her sister and eventually developed severe eating disorders. Looking back now, at the age of thirty, she can understand more clearly just what was going on during her long struggle to take charge of her life, but while she was living through it she suffered intensely, both mentally and physically. 'I felt I was living in a dream. I felt I wasn't really me. I used to have fantasies about who I would be and what I would look like. But it was all unreal. I was living in a vacuum, not in the real world, waiting to be me. I couldn't even explain what that meant, but I just knew that I wasn't me. It's only in the last few years I've been able to articulate how I felt then,' she explained.

The change to Beth's life was sudden and dramatic. She was three years younger than her sister Rebecca and the two girls were very different. Beth was something of a tomboy, outgoing and boisterous, while Rebecca was quieter and, at thirteen, beginning to get interested in clothes and make-up. Beth recalled those early years as being almost idyllic. 'I had a really happy childhood. I was very confident at school, I was popular and had lots of friends. We went on lots of family holidays. I was quite young for my age and I didn't really have any problems.'

Then one day, without any warning, Rebecca collapsed and died from a heart disorder which had never been diagnosed because, in her short life, she had never shown any signs of the condition. 'When I was told she was dead I screamed. I felt so angry. After that I think I just felt numb. It was too much to take in and I cut off my feelings altogether. When relatives and friends began arriving to comfort my parents, I remember feeling very separate from all these adults. There were no other children around and I felt very alone. All the focus was on the adults and no one was really noticing me. I felt quite detached from it all. I remember looking at the clock and thinking, "What are they all doing at school?", feeling I should be there and was missing out on something and then feeling guilty for thinking that.

'The next day I went back to school. I had a very supportive friend who sat with me in the playground, but the other kids would just come up and ask really direct questions about what had happened to my sister. I felt very separate and impotent. My best friend and I were very popular at school. When all this happened I felt a lot of shame and embarrassment. I felt very powerless and began to lose confidence in myself. The teachers had told the class, but the other kids didn't know how to deal with it, and I felt humiliated that I was being talked about. But none of the teachers said anything to me. There was no acknowledgement or support for what I was going through. They didn't know how to deal with it themselves. I think they felt embarrassed too. I remember being painfully aware of all this. It should have been acknowledged and it wasn't at all. Later on I began to go round with a sulky look on my face, so that they'd notice me and see I was upset. Then I'd feel guilty because it felt like pretending.

'The general message from everyone was, I felt, "Nothing has happened to you." I can't remember anyone validating what had happened to me. I was treated very much as a child, somebody who had to be protected. Everyone was very focused on the adults', not the child's, rights. Other people used to talk to me as if grief and loss were things I didn't understand and wasn't experiencing. Friends and neighbours used to ring up and say, "How's your Mum?" They never asked about me. Or they'd say, "Look after your Mum." None of them ever acknowledged that I'd lost a sister and I might be grieving too. It was as if I was someone who was totally outside the experience. One family friend used to say, "Be careful. Remember you're more precious now." I felt so uncomfortable with that. It might have been an innocent remark, but it felt so loaded with expectation about what I had to be and achieve now that my sister was gone. From very early on I felt I had to replace her. At school, everybody knew who was an only child. The only children in our class had loads of sweets and loads of attention. I had a real fear of becoming like them, being the only one, the only focus of attention.

'But I never voiced this to my parents. I felt very protective towards them and didn't want to worry them because of what they were going through. I felt a huge responsibility towards them right from the first day. I felt as if children have so many points, say twenty each, in terms of the stress they can cause their parents and that my sister had used up all hers and all mine in one go. I felt that I didn't have any left. That I couldn't do anything wrong because she'd used it all up by dying. I felt really trapped. Her death completely changed the family dynamics. I felt very angry with her for that, but I couldn't admit it to myself. I felt like I was living in a strait-jacket. I felt so much pressure.

'After Rebecca's death I also felt a lot of fear and terror. I was convinced that I was going to drop dead as well. I can remember lying in bed at night, sweating and in a total panic. I couldn't talk to my parents about how I was feeling because I was so worried about what they were going through. The fear of dying was very strong for me after Rebecca died and all through the years as I was growing up. I remember reaching the age she was when she died and believing I was going to die on that day. I felt a lot of guilt about living past her age. I felt that I shouldn't be alive because she wasn't.'

So, during the years immediately following her sister's death, Beth felt a mixture of guilt that she had survived, responsibility towards her parents, pressure from them to fulfil their expectations, and great insecurity. 'Until Rebecca died I had this feeling, like most kids, that your parents can make everything all right. With this, they couldn't do anything and it shattered my sense of security. I developed a lot of fear about the world and what can happen. I realized what it was like for it to be out of your control, to feel powerless. And I felt impotence that I couldn't make everything all right for my parents. I could see them going through all this and I couldn't do anything. I felt terribly lonely, growing up, and very isolated with all these feelings.

'Later on my parents and I used to have a lot of bad arguments. I felt a lot of anger towards them, but at the same time I used to worry all the time about what they were feeling. I used to go through a lot of turmoil about that. With people on the phone telling me to look after my Mum, I felt I should be supporting her. But I couldn't. We were locked in our own worlds really. I started to hate myself. I felt very inadequate all the time. I can remember people talking about my sister and feeling compared, feeling judged, feeling jealous, feeling "What about me?" There was such a lot of focus on this dead person. I always saw her as very good. It's hard to know how things would have been, but I feel I might have been rebellious anyway. She would have been the good one and I'd have been the naughty one. You can't get much better than dying at thirteen.

'I felt a lot of pressure to be like her and a lot of confusion about who I was. I began to feel my identity merging with hers and I fought very strongly against that. I felt a lot of anger, too, but you're not allowed to feel angry with somebody who's died. But it's inevitable. They've totally changed your life. I felt my childhood just went overnight. That feeling has stayed with me ever since and was a big contributory factor to my becoming anorexic. It was all about trying to get back to being this child of ten. I was stuck at being ten for a long time, stuck in the past really. I'm still working on that, that real "stuckness", wanting to be younger, wanting to be a child. It was all to do with memories of being on holiday on the beach, being carefree, running around, freedom. It all got tied up with my weight, but, basically, it was about the time when my sister was alive and life was easy and happy.

'I was very skinny when I was ten. Becoming thin was about trying to be a child again. It took me a long time to accept that the problem wasn't about being thin, but about wanting my family back from before. The anorexia started when I was about thirteen or fourteen. I felt very controlled by my parents. All the energy that had been put into two children got put into me. I started to reject food and I felt really good about that and in control. It built up to a head when I was about sixteen. Then it all swung the other way and I began bingeing. By the time I reached the age of eighteen I was very out of control around food and, in my desperation, I discovered bulimia. I found that I could eat huge amounts of food and then throw up to get rid of it all. I know now that what I was really throwing up was all the ugly, disgusting feelings I had never expressed. I had bulimia for a long, long time. It became very entrenched. It's very addictive behaviour and I've only recently let go of it.'

Looking back, Beth can see that she hardly grieved at all for the loss of her sister. She was dimly aware of the fact that she was bottling up her feelings of grief at the time, but didn't feel able to express them. When she went on to the secondary school where Rebecca had been a pupil, she became acutely conscious of what it meant not to have her big sister around. Again, as at her junior school, there was almost no mention by the teachers of the fact that she had only recently lost her sister. One teacher did make the remark, 'You're nothing like Rebecca, are you?', which Beth took to be an unfavourable comparison with her 'good' sister. Another teacher called her 'Rebecca' all the time and Beth never had the courage to say anything. On the recommendation of teachers from her junior school, she was also separated from her best friend on the grounds that they messed about and stopped each other from working. This friend had been very close and supportive, so the separation from her at the new school was another loss.

'I started to get quite argumentative at school. I was aggressive and used to have fights. I was quite disruptive really. At one point my parents got called to the school and afterwards I had to go and see the teacher. She said "You've got such caring parents. If you could only see some of the parents some of these children have." It reinforced the whole thing, that I was bad, that it was all my fault. Yet my behaviour was a cry for help and being admonished just reinforced all the guilt I already felt. I didn't get any support through this because it wasn't recognized. It just looked as if I was being a pain in the neck for no reason. I felt very insecure and very inadequate. I was so lonely, too. Not lonely for friends, but a deep inner loneliness that nothing could quell. I was having to deal with things that you don't normally have to deal with until you're an adult. Death. It's the "biggie". It's the bottom line. And being right on the edge of adolescence and all the changes you get with that made everything unbearable. All the time I was pretending I was OK, but inside I was living a nightmarish existence.

'Later I felt a lot of pressure about a career and what I was going to be. If my sister had been alive the interest would have been divided between us, but with her gone I felt all the hopes and ambitions for her were shifted on to me. If she had lived I'm sure it wouldn't have been all roses, but I wouldn't have had the same pressures. I felt I had to be two daughters, not one.'

With all the turmoil she was feeling inside, Beth found concentration at school difficult and left with few qualifications. Her eating problem got worse and eventually she went to her doctor, who referred her to a psychologist. It was Beth's first experience of any kind of therapy and it was not an auspicious start. Much later she worked with a therapist who helped her to get to the problems underlying her eating disorder, but with the first psychologist the main focus was on her overeating. 'I was given a diet sheet and told I needed will-power. My parents were asked to come to the second appointment, which was a disaster. We had this one session and it was worse than having none, because a lot of stuff came up and then when we got home we couldn't talk about it.'

Eventually, Beth left home and moved to another city where she shared a house with a group of people. 'Living in that house was a really important experience for me and I went through a lot of changes and realizations there. I had no boundaries or self-respect at first and I used to let some people walk all over me. But, slowly, things started to change and I began to like and accept myself more. After seven years I decided to move out and live on my own. I knew it was important but I couldn't have realized how crucial it was to my recovery. It's really helped me to connect with myself. The last two years have been a journey of discovery for me of what I really felt when Rebecca died.

'I started with a new therapist several years ago. I remember at the beginning thinking, "It's so huge I don't know where to start. It goes on for ever and ever." It was like seeing this whole sea swirling in front of me and not knowing where to begin. It all felt so messy. Writing has helped me. I've written poems and also diaries, which helped me to express my feelings. I had a really intensive reading period for a long time, mostly self-help books and books on childhood trauma and recovery. They really helped. Seeing exactly what I felt written down in print really validated my experience. It helped me believe in myself and inspired me to keep going. Not long after I began living on my own, I became ill for a while and couldn't do anything. That whole experience of feeling powerless threw me straight into grief. It was incredible. So many feelings of loss came up. They were exactly the feelings I must have had when Rebecca died and which I had never expressed. This time, though, I got it all out. I had to work through it. Looking back now, I feel it was like being given a second chance to grieve for her and for my lost child.

'I know now that my eating problem was an attempt to regain my old self and to make a stand for who I am, when I felt really moulded by those around me. It became an outlet for everything that I never expressed and never felt and never grieved for. Anger, shame, guilt, sadness, everything was expressed through food. That was why it had such a hold on me and was so hard to give up. It was very addictive. There were times when I just didn't think I was going to live. Parts of my diary say things like "I feel like I'm rotting inside. I'm dying inside." It was like a slow suicide. I think that was another part of it. "I shouldn't be here, but I'm not allowed to die, so I'll do it indirectly."

'The relationship with my parents now is very different. In many ways it seems renewed. It feels on a different level. I feel more adult with them. There is respect in the relationship now on both sides. I realize that I'm actually very close to them and I don't need to kick against that any more. There's no one in my life now who knew my sister, except for them, and because of what we've all been through there is a very strong bond. I feel the relationship changing and I really value that.

'The relationship with my sister just got cut off and it's only in the last couple of years that I've started connecting with that. When I was thirty I wanted to do something really meaningful, so I went on my own to the Orkneys. I'd wanted to go there for a long time. It felt really important to go on my own. It was only when I got there and was on the boat that I suddenly felt really connected to my sister. It was the first time I'd ever felt that and it felt very spiritual. Those feelings and connections stayed with me for the rest of my time there. It was a very emotional time. I found this deserted beach and had this ritual. It was very powerful. I have a little ritual on the anniversary of her death now and on her birthday, whereas before I just used to feel hideous and terrible. I let myself cry now and feel her loss and it's very intense. Her death left a huge gap in my life and I miss her terribly, but I'm making peace with my past. I feel I'm nearer the end of the journey, but I'm at the beginning of connecting with it all.'

NOTE

1. Paul contacted me some months later to say that he had moved on since the interview. He said that talking about his brother's death and its effect on his life had been part of that moving-on process. He had begun to feel more accepting of events and more able to deal with the feelings of powerlessness.

CHAPTER 16
Out of the shadow

The shadow cast by the death of a child in a family will touch everybody. Whether or not the individual members continue to live in the gloom of that shadow depends very much on how much 'healthy' grieving they are permitted to do in the weeks, months and years immediately following the death. There *are* routes out of the shadow into the sunshine of happier days. The shadow may still be there, but the bereaved, if they are fortunate enough to have space in which to come to terms with their loss, will find ways of incorporating it. To use another metaphor, the wounds will heal, a scab will grow over them. The scab may be knocked occasionally and the wounds will open up again, but, for most of the time, the person will be able to get on with his or her life, suffering only occasional pain from the sore place.

Forty-five years is a long time to go on suffering the pain of a bereavement. Jean Howlett, who is now fifty-eight, lost one of her brothers when she was coming up to her thirteenth birthday. While recalling those past events she broke down and wept several times. 'There are various recognized stages for grieving, aren't there? I know I've read about it,' she said. 'But I don't think any of us went through it. Not as we should have done, anyway. I'm still stuck in the first part. I feel as if the wound has never healed. It's always raw. And it shouldn't be so. Not for all that time.'

Jean was the eldest of three children, born when her mother was thirty-six and her father forty-six. Eighteen months later Ian was born, followed in less than two years by Alan. The children were much loved and well cared for and those early years of childhood were very happy. During the summer of 1949 Jean was sent to stay with relatives in Scotland for six weeks. She had always loved staying away from home with these particular relations and went away quite cheerfully. Three weeks later, Ian, the brother she was most close to, contracted meningitis.

'I was told he was ill. I thought he had sunstroke, because that's what was said at first. But my mother knew, or suspected, anyway.

She couldn't be a trained children's nurse and not know. But it wasn't mentioned to me. I think maybe they were trying to shelter me, especially as I was on my own in Scotland and would be travelling back on my own. I didn't feel shut out at that stage. I came home about three weeks later and by then Ian was in St Thomas's Hospital in London, desperately ill. I hadn't seen him since I went to Scotland and I didn't see him again. It was difficult when I got home because my parents were travelling up and down from Wandsworth to see him. They were often called at night, I found out later. He would seem to be fading away and the hospital would ring a neighbour downstairs and she would come and sit with us. They'd be back again in the morning, Ian having survived the night, and Alan and I never even knew. I think it would have been better if we had known. But I can remember my mother saying one day, "Ian isn't going to get better. He's going to die." She did say that. So I was warned. But it was still terrible when it happened.'

Jean cannot remember why she was never taken to see Ian in hospital. She thought perhaps the hospital regulations in 1949 were much stricter about not permitting child visitors. Apparently, Alan, then aged nine, was taken to the hospital one day, but was not allowed to see his brother. 'He said he could hear Ian crying with pain, so I don't think visiting him would have been a pleasant experience anyway. I don't know now if I wish I could have gone. But I wasn't allowed to go to the funeral either. That was my headmistress's decision. My mother had written a letter telling the school that Ian had died and asking if I could have the day off for the funeral. The headmistress opened the letter, read it and said, "I'm sorry." I can remember going back to the class-room, howling away, and the form mistress asked what was wrong. Somebody said, "Her brother died on Friday" and she thought the girl had said, "Her mother died", so there was confusion over that. I got through the day somehow and I had a letter from the headmistress to take home. In it she said she didn't think it would be a good idea for me to attend the funeral. So I didn't go. I had no chance to say goodbye.'

Jean said her parents never got over Ian's death. Nor did she. 'We didn't talk about him, because it was so desperately difficult for my parents. I think they just shut him away. So, of course, we had to as well. Alan and I had to carry on with my mother in the most awful state. She managed to get a job as a nurse in a department store and I think really that's what kept her going. The only time we kept in touch with the fact that Ian had died was when Daddy used to take Alan and me out to the cemetery on a Sunday morning. I don't remember my mother ever going. Ian wasn't talked about at home. And that's what was wrong. We handled it wrongly. We should have kept him alive in our memories, our thoughts, by talking about him. It was as though he hadn't lived. It was as though it was so painful we'd got to pretend that it had never happened, that he had never lived. I mean we all knew and we were all suffering, but we just kept quiet to avoid people feeling more hurt. Whether my parents talked about it among themselves when Alan and I weren't there I don't know. But we didn't talk as a family, we survived individually. I felt shut into my own grief.'

Jean's relationship with her surviving brother was also difficult. 'We were already at loggerheads. For some reason or other I was jealous of Alan. I think that's partly because I was sent away to stay with somebody else when he was born. After Ian died I can remember Alan and I saying to one another, "I wish it was you that had died." That's horrendous, isn't it? We're OK with each other now, but it affected our childhood. I think my parents could have looked out for things like that. I know Alan missed Ian dreadfully, but I think in a way he coped with it all better because he was around all the time through the summer. I was shut away from it all. Alan seems to have been able to express his feelings a bit more. It hasn't affected him for so long. He cried when my father told us that Ian had died. I'll never forget the sound of Alan crying. Eventually we all gathered in the sitting-room. The neighbour who'd looked after us was there. She came over and put her arm round my mother. We were all sitting in the dark, with just the firelight. We just sat there quietly in the dark and that was the only time I can remember us all being together in our grief.'

Jean said that both she and her mother, now in her nineties, were still incapable of talking about Ian without weeping. 'I think crying is all right, but not if it gets in the way constantly, which it does for me. Look, I'm crying now. It shouldn't happen like this. Not after forty-five years. I think bereaved people need to get through a sort of pain barrier and cry and howl and create and sob. I don't think I've ever done that. My mother and I are so inhibited. And I never saw my father cry, never. I think he withdrew into himself a great deal. I don't think either of my parents understood about talking about feelings. My mother told me once that if people stopped her when she was out shopping to say how sorry they were about Ian's death she couldn't stand it. She had to run home. I think it's too late now to talk to her about Ian. I'd like to, but I don't feel I can upset her at her age.'

One of the main effects on Jean of her brother's death was anxiety about leaving her parents. On the surface, she said, she got over Ian's loss and carried on with her own life. 'I was happy at school and had masses of friends. I had the Church. I had the tennis club, boy-friends. There was lots going on. But when it came down to the nitty-gritty, to making big decisions, the decisions I should have made about my life, I lost confidence. My school was doing everything it could to get me to go to university. I was even taken to Cambridge and shown round by the headmistress. She did everything she could to persuade me, and I wouldn't do it. I'm sure I wouldn't do it because I was afraid of leaving home. And I was afraid because of Ian. Something had happened when I was away and I was afraid it would happen again. I don't think my parents realized that. They wanted me to go. But it was my decision not to. I should have gone to university. Instead I retreated into marriage and lived very close to my parents. When we moved to Folkestone my parents came too and my mother has lived with me now for thirty-odd years. I've only ever lived about four years of my entire life without my mother being there. I know it's something to do with Ian's death. It's not being able to let go of the fear of something happening if I'm not there. I love my mother dearly and I feel responsible for her.'

Jean also said that she felt she had been over-protective of her own children, a son and a daughter. When she and her husband divorced she was overcome with feelings of guilt, because she felt her daughter suffered a great deal from the breakup. This reinforced her feelings of responsibility and further dented her self-confidence. 'My parents were destroyed by Ian's death to a great extent. If he hadn't died I think they would have been quite different, and so life would have been very different for me. It was all so confidence-sapping. Well, you can see how uptight I am about it. I would have gone to university. I wouldn't have married so young. I'm not intellectually fulfilled. People say it's never too late and I do feel ready now for some space for myself, more than ready. But I've got commitments. I have wondered about having some counselling, but I think, "What's the point now?" I know what's caused my problems. If there had been somebody there at the time, even a neighbour or an aunty, it might have helped. But there was nobody.'

When I asked Betty Rathbone about delayed or uncompleted mourning processes she explained that for those who hadn't done 'enough work', as she put it, at the time of the bereavement, there was always a risk of it catching up with them later. 'You can't say that it necessarily will, but you can say that there's always a risk. In my work we're sometimes dealing with something which is well back in the past, but won't lie down. Sometimes, apparently, it hasn't caused any problem for years, but some change in life circumstances will make it all come alive again. Perhaps a similar sort of thing happening a second time, or maybe another bereavement which, in itself, shouldn't be so massively important, taps into the old buried grief. A person may be coming up with an apparently pathological reaction to, say, the death of a pet, but the reason for this is that a lot of the feelings don't actually belong there, they belong to the earlier situation. The new circumstances have triggered them off. So somebody who hasn't done enough work at the time is going to be at risk of being confronted with the extra work to do when some other loss occurs.'

For Barbara Talmage, a long-delayed reaction to the death of her brother came about as the result of another bereavement. Not the comparatively minor loss of a pet or of somebody not particularly close, but the suicide of her older daughter at the age of twenty-three. The nightmare of her daughter's death drove Barbara 'out of my head' as she described it, a terrible, bleak and desperate state in which grief and guilt over the tragedy of her daughter were mixed up with anger and pain over the loss of her brother more than thirty years before.

During those three decades, Barbara said she always felt shut off from the rest of the world, as if she was behind glass. At school she was disruptive and antisocial, she never trusted adults and always felt she was acting a part. The complete loss of control, in the wake of her daughter's death, was devastating. Eventually she turned to a professional psychotherapist for a lengthy period of individual counselling sessions, out of which came a new sense of wholeness and well-being. 'When that glass was broken down and shattered I thought, "I can be me. I can say whatever I like. I can be angry. I can cry. I don't have to pretend any more." Before, I had spent years blocking everything off and was never totally relaxed.'

Barbara is now forty-seven. She lives outside Oxford with her husband Allen and teenage daughter Vicky. Lucy, her first daughter, born when Barbara was a college student and unmarried, died three years ago. Until Lucy's death triggered off a complete breakdown, followed by a painful process of recovery, Barbara had always regarded herself as the black sheep of her family. She was fourth in a family of seven girls and one boy, Peter, who was eighteen months older than her. The two were very close. When they were younger they shared a bedroom and used to talk together before they went to sleep. The family had lived in Hong Kong for several years, but in the spring of 1958, when Barbara was eleven, plans were made to return to England. Peter had already been sent to live with their maternal grandparents in Kent, where he was going to school.

'So I actually said goodbye to Peter in Hong Kong, although I can't remember it. We all came back later and went to live in Teignmouth. Peter was due to come and see us in a school holiday; I'm not sure if it was Easter or Whitsun. But the weekend before that he was knocked off his bike and killed. I can remember my Dad telling us. Mum couldn't say anything. He gathered us all together – I can see it now, I was sort of squatted on the floor – and he was terribly upset. He said, "Peter's had an accident." And it didn't sink in that he meant Peter. I thought he meant a person called Peters. So, in my innocence, I said, "Who's Peters?" He got all upset and hit me. Then he told us that our brother Peter had died. I don't know what happened next. But none of us went to the funeral and we hardly ever talked about him again. My mother couldn't even say his name for years and years. I learned later that her mother had told her she must be brave and carry on. And, apparently, at the funeral my Nanny said to my Dad, "Oh, stop crying." Nanny took over and organized the funeral and everything. The children mustn't come, mustn't see anything, mustn't see his body, mustn't say goodbye. We were totally blocked out.'

Soon after Peter's death the whole family moved from Devon to Deal, where Peter was buried. 'I didn't think this at the time, but it was to go and be near him. And, even though we never ever talked about him, we often went round to his grave. My mother actually uprooted the whole family for that. But, to my knowledge, she never cried about Peter. And my father never said a word about him. He was a quiet man, anyway. He was in the Air Force and used to go away a lot, so Mum was really the boss at home. There was one aunty I could talk to about Peter. She wasn't a real aunty but we called her Aunty Peggy. She was an old friend of my Mum's, a single lady. She didn't have any children of her own, but she was very understanding. She was the only person I could talk to, but she didn't live near us and only came to stay about once a year.'

Barbara was sent off to a convent boarding-school. After the freedom of life in Hong Kong, where the children had spent all their spare time on the beach, and coming so soon after her brother's death, school life was unbearable. 'I was naughty all the time. I was really disruptive, pushing the nuns as far as I could and behaving dreadfully. I'm sure it was because of all this pain inside. But nobody sorted me out. I remember once, in a geography exam of all things, I started writing about Peter. It all came tumbling out. I wrote pages and pages. The nuns just took it in, but nobody said a word. I mean, somebody must have read it. You cry for help and nobody hears. It's awful. I suppose those feelings got buried in the end and I just carried on. I changed myself, mentally, into being the third instead of the fourth in the family. I never said I had a brother. I never mentioned him.'

Barbara left school at age sixteen, although her mother wanted her to stay on. She tried nursing for a while, but found the discipline hard to take. Later she decided to train as a teacher and began to enjoy life as a student. She was still at college when she became pregnant with Lucy.

'Everybody advised me to give her away, forget about it and carry on with my training. That's what unmarried people were supposed to do in those days. I had her placed with foster-parents, but when I finished college I felt as if I had this big hole inside me, so I took her back. It felt like the first big decision that I'd ever made. I'd kept in touch a bit, while she was being fostered, but not enough really. Looking back, I think Lucy was very unsettled and upset by being moved away, but it was what I wanted at the time. She was a lovely kid.'

Barbara struggled along for several years as a single parent. Then, when Lucy was nine, she married Allen, a very supportive man with a young son of his own, who willingly took on the role of stepfather. Vicky was born and, over the years, she and Lucy developed a close relationship. However, as she reached her late teens and early adulthood, Lucy started to suffer from severe bouts of depression. She spent some time in a psychiatric hospital and went through a phase of wanting to have nothing to do with her family. After prolonged treatment she was considered well enough to be moved to a half-way house and it was there that she took the overdose of paracetamol which killed her.

The shock to Barbara was appalling, but for a few weeks after Lucy's death she somehow managed to keep going. Allen was a tower of strength. 'He did everything. Well, we just all went round together as a family, but Allen did all the sorting out. I made a point of involving Vicky in all the processes, asking her what she thought, what hymn she wanted at the funeral, if she wanted to choose a reading. I did the things I felt I had to do. Allen's son David was coming up to his eighteenth birthday and I managed to keep strong for his party. After that I just collapsed. I couldn't cope any longer. I had no capacity left to worry about anybody else. I knew I had to get away.'

Barbara left home and went to stay with a woman friend. 'She was great. She just left me alone. I don't know what I would have done without her. She just let me do whatever I wanted to do. I wouldn't talk to anybody on the phone. I took to wandering round the graveyard trying to find out who all the people were, looking for all the children's graves. I didn't know what I was doing it for. I used to wander round the hospital where Lucy had been a patient. I couldn't work. Everything was black, all black and horrible. I hadn't wanted to keep any of Lucy's clothes, but I had all her soaps and shampoos. I remember I used to wash and wash and wash, thinking if I could use up all the soap, the pain would be gone. I knew it was mad, yet I carried on. I was totally out of my head for about two months. My friend was brilliant. She never said a word to stop me.'

When Barbara returned home she had come through the worst of her breakdown, but she realized she needed help. Another bereaved parent had told her about The Compassionate Friends (see Chapter 8) and she contacted the local organizer. 'I just phoned her up and she was so gentle. I cried my heart out over the phone. Then she wrote me a couple of nice letters and I started going to meetings. I couldn't speak for the first few meetings. I just sat there crying the whole time. We'd never been allowed to cry at home as children.'

On the advice of friends she had made at The Compassionate Friends, Barbara then decided to go for counselling. 'I'd always had this thing about not wanting to be a patient, not wanting to have any treatment. I didn't want to do it for a long while, but I just felt so awful I knew I had to do something to get myself better. My counsellor was very good. Apart from a few lead-up questions at the beginning when she asked me to tell her about my family, she never asked questions about anything. She just sat there and listened to whatever I wanted to talk about. And then everything started to come out; it all started unwinding somehow. While I was seeing her I started having nightmares and weird dreams. I remember one dream in which I was shut in this room, with a great big lock on the door. I was gradually opening the lock and coming out, but when I came through that door there was a big glass door in the way. That was really significant. I'd always felt I was seeing the world from behind glass. Through counselling I had to shatter that glass and let my real self out. I had blocked so much. A lot of it was about Peter's death. I started crying about him for the first time. And I decided to go to his grave again. I had to go back years and years to think where it was; I'd only been a kid the last time I went there. Allen came with me; he was very supportive. We scrubbed the gravestone and I said goodbye to Peter. At about that time I went to the funeral of another child and I cried and cried and cried. It felt good to do that.'

Barbara said she had been amazed when all these powerful feelings came up. She had no idea they were there, so successfully had she suppressed them for years and years. 'You see, we never talked about feelings at home. My Mum still doesn't tell you how she feels about anything. I think she's very repressed and nervous. She talks about pulling yourself together. That's how she goes on. She's telling herself really. I've started talking to her about Peter but she can only manage that for a little while. Now, as a bereaved parent, I talk about Lucy quite a lot. We all do. I think about her birthday and the day she died. But I've never heard my mother say anything like that about Peter. All Peter's stuff disappeared too. I would have liked to have had something of his. He was mad about torches and I would liked to have had one of his torches, something that I could have taken to bed and hugged. We never had pictures of him about the house either, but I've got my mother to send me some now and I have them out on show with pictures of Lucy.'

Once her initial crisis was over, Barbara also turned her attention to Vicky, who had become very depressed. 'I went with her to the doctor, a woman who had known Lucy, and it was heart-breaking when Vicky started telling her how she wasn't sleeping very well, wasn't eating properly, had no friends. I had been feeling so awful myself I hadn't noticed what was going on. So we started from there really. Although we'd included her in all the arrangements after Lucy died I'd never asked her how she felt. It turned out she had felt left out when Allen and I went to see Lucy in hospital – she was on a life-support machine at first. And she'd been distressed, imagining Lucy actually taking the overdose. I hope she's talked it all through now. She went to art therapy for a while and that seemed to help. I know I feel totally different. I feel as if I'm myself now. I didn't know who I was for a long, long time.'

CHAPTER 17
Secrets in the family

The strain placed on children in families in which a sibling death has taken place is severe. It is made worse when the adults involved discourage any references to the dead child, either by avoiding the subject themselves or by becoming so upset at any mention of his or her name that the surviving children fear they will cause further distress by talking to them about it. Those unspoken taboos are very powerful and, as we have seen from earlier chapters, children are very good at picking up clues from their parents as to what the appropriate behaviour must be. If, within the family, it appears that nothing must be said about the child who has died, they will abide by these rules. If they are lucky, they may find somebody outside the immediate family circle to whom they can express their thoughts and feelings, ask questions and experience the comfort of talking it through. Within the family, however, they will keep quiet.

When a dead child is erased from conversation, when photographs are hidden away, it seems almost as if that child never existed. Where is the evidence of his or her having lived? Where are the reminders of who he or she was? How can the memories be sustained if they cannot be given voice? If the child died when a sibling was very young and that information has been stored away as a secret in the family, what effect will it have when the survivor learns the truth?

Mary P. (Chapter 14) told me of the sadness she felt when, for an essay on the theme of personal experience, one of her pupils said she had wanted to write about the shock of discovering that she was one of twins, but her mother had forbidden her to do so. It turned out that the child's grandmother, before her death, had shown the girl a photograph of the twins as toddlers. Although shocked by the news the girl was also relieved, because it confirmed her inner conviction that she had, indeed, had a close playmate when she was small. When the grandmother died the photograph disappeared, and the girl's mother denied that it had ever existed. She also denied the existence of the twin and told her daughter that she didn't want the matter to be discussed any further.

Julian Batchelor comes from a family riddled with taboos. From his earliest memories there had always been certain subjects which were never aired by his parents, and therefore never talked about by the children either. The biggest taboo was the death of his twin sister at the age of two-and-a-half. Such was the strict adherence to the family rules of secrecy that he was eleven before he heard about her for the first time. The news left him completely stunned. Worse still, he felt quite unable to pursue the subject and was left with countless unanswered questions and troubled emotions. At thirty, he is still only marginally nearer to resolving the situation.

Before telling me about his discovery that he had once had a twin sister, Julian, who is a professional musician, explained what he called 'the historical background' to his family's conspiracy of silence. He had found out, comparatively recently, that the man he had always believed to be his father's cousin was, in fact, his father's half-brother. Julian's paternal grandmother had given birth to two illegitimate children when she was a very young girl, one of whom had died. The other, who survived, had always been known in the family as a cousin. The facts only came to light after the grandmother died. 'Both the death and the illegitimacy were hushed up for years,' said Julian. 'It seems to be a family pattern. What happened in my case is that my twin sister died when we were two-and-a-half. That's about as much as I know really.'

Julian and his twin sister were born when his two older sisters were seven and thirteen. Despite the family taboo, he has managed to piece together a few scraps of information about his early life, but it remains very sketchy. 'Apparently, I was the one not expected to survive of the two children and I nearly didn't. Very shortly after she died I was taken into hospital, with croup or something, and was in an oxygen tent for nearly a month. It must have been quite unbearable for my parents. And, of course, my older sisters would have been very well aware of my twin's death and must have been very distressed by it. I have some extremely shadowy, very, very vague memories of my twin sister being with me. But after that time I have no memories of what occurred next. My next memories are of when I was about four. There's a huge gap. I was really quite stunned when I found out about my twin. I must have been about eleven. It was at the dinner table. One of my sisters mentioned it. We were just sitting there, eating. It was a very awkward moment, a blunder, because she was breaking the taboo. She said, "You know, Julian, you had a twin sister." I said, "What?" and she said, "You had a sister and she died." I was so taken aback I didn't know what to say. I didn't know what to do.'

Was this an opening for further revelations? Apparently not. The subject was dropped. Nobody around the table said another word, not even the sister who had dared to mention it in the first place. 'No. The extent of the taboo is that it makes itself into a conspiracy. Everybody takes it on board. The atmosphere never feels right in the rather peculiar dynamics of my family. I've tried asking about it on a number of different occasions, but I've been fobbed off. I've been told it's never been the right time to ask. And I feel awkward about it. I feel I've taken the taboo on board and that's part of the problem. After that occasion, when my sister said that at the dinner table, it was never mentioned again. I had no access to any photographs of my twin. I don't know what her name was. I stumbled across a couple of pictures once, by mistake, ones they hadn't hidden, I suppose. I have a niece who looks very much like my sister did in those photographs, from what I remember of them. That must be hard for my mother, I think, but I don't know. She's never said.'

Julian went on to explain that it was only recently that he had begun to ponder on the lack of openness in his family. As a child growing up in such a closed atmosphere, he had accepted it almost without question. As an adult, he had begun to see things differently and recognized that the secrecy about his twin was only one of many guarded areas.

'I feel that my family are a bit of a closed book. I wasn't close to my oldest sister. I didn't grow up with her really. I hardly remember her being at home. I get on with her fairly well now and I think I could broach the subject of my twin sister with her, were the opportunity there. She's married, with four daughters, and she shares quite a lot of the very same frustrations that I have about my parents and finds their tightness, their lack of approachability on emotionally important subjects very hard to bear. I think it's possible I could talk to her. With my middle sister I'm not sure. We got on extraordinarily well when I was a child. We used to sing together all the time and really work at it. We used to do lots of harmony singing and we were very good at it. Then my voice broke and I was fairly useless to her. And she started some fairly serious bullying. I got very badly abused by her over a period of about three or four years. It was pretty horrific. I couldn't talk to my parents about it. It struck me, just now, talking about it, that there was a very violent side to that abuse, a vindictiveness. And it makes me wonder whether, in some strange way, I was somehow being held responsible for the death of the child, that I was being punished, made the scapegoat. In our family there can't have been much of a climate for her to deal with her feelings about the death.'

As for his parents, Julian admitted he was frightened of forcing any kind of emotional upset. 'You see, I do get on with them fairly well on one level. When I see them it usually takes a few days for me to relax into it and cease to be irritated. But I'm not comfortable enough to be able to spoil that equilibrium and ask questions which might upset or embarrass them. They may have been trying to protect me in the past; now I'm trying to protect them. We're all trying to protect each other. And there's so much there. Years of hidden stuff. Emotional issues have been completely avoided; anything emotionally meaningful in any way has not been dealt with at all.

'My mother came from a working-class Jewish ghetto in the East End of London. Total poverty in the Twenties and Thirties. Her father was a complete waster, an inveterate layabout. She feels a lot of guilt about that. She's tried to construct a bourgeois life which is absolutely nothing to do with the real her. I was sent away to a public school when I was thirteen, which was a peculiar thing, because it was something my parents had no experience of. And, of course, that was a very closed environment. Emotional things, more than ever, couldn't be talked about unless you managed to find an ally in another chap at school. It was completely barren as far as I was concerned. There was fagging and a lot of bullying. It was ghastly really. Therefore, none of those key emotional points in your life – going through puberty, talking about sex – none of that was ever tackled. It's still the same in my relationship with my parents. When we speak on the phone it's just an exchange of news. It's nothing to do with how we are.

'I think my parents invested a lot of hope and, I suppose, some kind of faith in me. I always, always was told how important it was for me to do something really important. Initially it was going to be something respectable. Then it was going to be something slightly less respectable, as they saw it. And that was going to be singing in opera. They desperately wanted me to do that and they helped me a lot. I haven't quite done what they wanted me to do, partly deliberately, I know. So I feel I've been a source of disappointment to them as well. If I trusted myself more I might be able to try and sort things out with them, and it would probably help them tremendously to open up to me. But I'm not ready yet.'

However, Julian has begun to deal with some of the backlog of concealed emotional baggage. He's had some counselling and also tried Gestalt therapy, concerning himself primarily with what he felt were more pressing matters than the loss of his twin sister. The taboo about her death was only one aspect of the problem with secrets in the family. He said he had leapt at the chance to talk about her to me and had been seriously considering hypnotherapy as a means of recalling facts about her.

'It would be a very good thing for me to stop ignoring, to address it further and to take a bit more control and responsibility. I've been seeing an acupuncturist and he says there's an emotional part of me which suffers terrible blockages. When I think about it, there's a pain in my chest virtually all the time. I'm sure a lot of this stuff is bound up in that. It would be better to let go. I'm not conscious of much regret about her death, but occasionally it strikes me how lovely it would be to have a twin sister. I try to imagine the different course my life would have taken had she been around. And I still dream about her an awful lot. Sometimes she's a little girl, sometimes she's the same age as me and sometimes she's being introduced as somebody who is my twin but who I haven't seen for a long time. But she's invariably great. That is the thing. She's invariably really, really good. Usually in the dream she's laughing or she's happy. That's actually rather lovely.'

CHAPTER 18
Resolution

The stories told by the people in this book speak for themselves. Each one has an individual viewpoint, each its own voice. Yet, despite the wide differences in the ages of the people concerned, not only when they had suffered the loss of a sibling but also when they were recalling the tragedy, there is a remarkable similarity in the accounts they have given. Significant, too, is the clarity of recall. While there were certain gaps in memory, most of those concerned had vivid recollections of the events they had witnessed and the feelings which those events had aroused. All had suffered, not just from the loss of the sibling, but from the changes in family life which the death had precipitated.

What can be learned from their experiences? Indeed, what must be learned, if future generations of bereaved children are to be spared some of the traumas which have been explored here?

Of course, with the reductions in infant mortality rates this century, it is unlikely that we shall see again the sheer numbers of children dying which our Victorian forebears were obliged to regard as commonplace. They had little option but to accept that children were susceptible to certain illnesses for which they had no cure and which were likely to prove fatal. We live in an age which has developed vaccines to counteract former killer–illnesses among the young and, almost daily, we read of new cures and remarkable life-saving techniques. To some extent, this exacerbates the problem of childhood death. We don't expect it in the way that previous generations did, and certainly not from illnesses. Parents today are more likely to be fearful of road accidents than they are of most childhood diseases. Even so, when a child dies, we are so shocked, so unpractised in responding to such a loss, that we reel back in disbelief. If adults find it so difficult to come to terms with the death of a child, then how much more difficult it must be for children, for whom the whole concept of death itself is, in any case, not part of what might be called their 'life curriculum'.

Betty Rathbone said she believed that very few people are

comfortable in the presence of somebody who has had a significant loss, and that when it's a question of the death of a child the problem is even worse. 'People literally don't know what to say, so they'll cross the road rather than confront the situation.'

However, as the bereaved siblings in this book have indicated, those who have lost someone close to them want the enormity of that loss to be acknowledged. Onlookers of such a tragedy may feel completely inadequate. How can they possibly say anything which might be helpful, something which doesn't sound banal? Will they upset the bereaved person by referring to the death? The truth of the matter is that the bereaved person is upset anyway. Whatever is said cannot make the situation worse, but an acknowledgement will at least indicate that the relative, friend or acquaintance recognizes the pain of the situation. As Annie Richards (Chapter 7) said, she just wanted people to say something, no matter how crass or inadequate. Without this acknowledgement she felt like an alien.

It is clear that one of the most significant differences between adults and children in their handling of the mourning process is that adults are in charge of their own lives. John Bowlby, writing about children's mourning, with particular reference to the death of a parent,[1] puts it this way:

> Many differences arise from the fact that a child is even less his own master than is a grown-up. For example, whereas an adult is likely either to be present at the time of a death or else to be given prompt and detailed information about it, in most cases a child is entirely dependent for his information on the decision of his surviving relatives: and he is in no position to institute inquiries as an adult would should he be kept in the dark.
>
> In a similar way, a child is at an even greater disadvantage than is an adult should his relatives or other companions prove unsympathetic to his yearning, his sorrow and his anxiety. For, whereas an adult can, if he wishes, seek further for understanding and comfort should his first exchanges prove unhelpful, a child is rarely in a position to do so. Thus some at least of the differences between the mourning of children and the mourning of adults are due to a child's life being even less within his control than is that of a grown-up.
>
> Other problems arise from a child having even less knowledge and understanding of issues of life and death than has an adult. In consequence he is more apt to make false inferences from the information he receives and also to misunderstand the significance of events he observes and remarks he overhears. Figures of speech in

particular are apt to mislead him. As a result it is necessary for the adults caring for a bereaved child to give him even more opportunity to discuss what has happened and its far-reaching implications than it is with an adult.

It is significant that Bowlby uses the word 'necessary'. It is necessary that some adult steps in to give the bereaved child the help and support he or she needs. Children bereaved of a sibling are at a particular disadvantage, in that the adults who would normally be helping them to come to terms with a deeply disturbing experience, that is, the parents, are themselves not in a fit state, certainly in the immediate aftermath of the death, to see beyond their own overwhelming grief and despair. But that supportive person does not have to be the parent. It can be an aunt, a family friend, a teacher. Someone stable, accessible and willing to answer questions honestly. Someone who will allow the child space in which to deal with whatever feelings are coming up, without passing judgement on them.

Experts in reactions to bereavement agree that there is a predictable pattern to the process of coming to terms with it. The survivor will experience a range of emotions, usually starting with shock and, possibly, disbelief. Anger, guilt and grief are likely to follow, not necessarily in that order and often all mixed up together. If the person is allowed to express these feelings, a 'healthy' mourning process will be achieved and he or she will move forward into an acceptance of the loss. Children, just as much as adults, need support and understanding from those around them in order to work through this process. In addition, they will need more in the way of explanations. Adults know about the realities of death, the necessary rites and rituals that go with it. Children do not.

How these explanations are made is a matter of individual judgement. Much will depend on the age of the surviving siblings, but even young children can be helped to cope with the reality of losing a brother or sister if given straightforward information in simple terms, rather than being fobbed off with confusing half–truths or, worse still, left out of the picture altogether. 'I think attitudes are changing,' said Betty Rathbone, 'but it certainly used to be thought humane to protect children from any nastiness, so they were more or less totally excluded from the process. There are obvious difficulties about involving very small children, but even older children very often get put to one side deliberately. But the death affects the whole family and has to be coped with as a reality.

If the necessary information isn't available to children, then imagination has to take over and, mostly, the imagination is far worse than the reality. Where the details are very painful, I think, sometimes, people don't know how to speak about it and therefore they say nothing. I think then a simplified version is what is required. Children don't need to have a blow-by-blow account as it were. But they do need to have a story which makes sense, not a story with gaps in it.'

Many surviving siblings have expressed regret at not being allowed to attend the funeral. They felt they had missed out on an important rite of passage. Ann Howard (see Chapter 13) felt cheated because she didn't go to her baby sister's funeral, even though she understood that her parents were probably trying to protect her from a possibly harrowing experience. In Betty Rathbone's opinion, attending the funeral helps to make the death real, but she also believes that the child needs to be supported. 'If the parent is completely collapsed and unable to support the child and there's nobody else around to help, then I think it can be totally overwhelming. In that sort of situation I think it's a good thing if you can find an aunt or a family friend, who is able to be with the child and to deal with the child's feelings. If the parents are disabled from doing that, as they may well be, somebody known to the family, somebody caring, can help to steady the child through the experience.'

Bereaved parents, however distraught, may make a tremendous effort to shield their remaining children from the powerful emotions which such a death produces. It is natural to wish to protect one's offspring from pain, but children are like sponges; they soak up the atmosphere, and will sense their parents' grief even if it is not openly expressed or shared. Not being told directly what their parents are suffering can cause great anxiety to a sensitive child, who will put his or her own construction on the situation and imagine scenarios which, however divorced from reality, will make some sort of sense. Francesca Blythe (Chapter 9) thought her mother would have preferred it if she had died instead of her sister. Mary P. (Chapter 14) believed her parents had gone mad and that her brother wasn't dead at all.

So, should parents just let go and forget about the effect of their behaviour on the rest of the family? Should they feel free to weep and wail, rant and rave? There are no easy answers to these questions, but from the evidence of the people in this book it would appear that open expressions of grief are probably easier for children to deal with than stony silences. When parents block their emotions children follow suit, and the whole family becomes locked in a web of unresolved mourning, the effects of which may haunt them for years.

On the other hand, there is no need for parents to involve their remaining children in every outpouring of woe. Children can become very distressed when they witness adults crying and will need to be reassured that this is a way of relieving the pain. They also need to be helped to understand that grief over the death of their sibling can be triggered quite unexpectedly and they don't have to tiptoe around, watching everything they say or do in order not to upset their parents. As Betty Rathbone pointed out, children are very self-absorbed. It is all too easy for them to feel responsible for tempering the emotional climate. The healthy side of that self-absorption means, also, that they will want their parents to put their mourning to one side for some of the time at least and give attention to the concerns and activities of the surviving children.

Those whose parents never talked about the dead child were horrified at this apparent blotting out of that sibling's existence. 'We never talked about him or her' was a recurring complaint. Yet, even when the dead child *is* talked about, there are pitfalls. June Wilde (Chapter 3) submerged her own personality in a futile attempt to become like her eulogized dead sister, eventually growing to resent the very mention of this perfect sibling's name. 'The child who has died prematurely very often becomes, as it were, the sainted child,' said Betty Rathbone. 'The silly things, the naughty things are forgotten and all the desirable characteristics are remembered, so that the live child can never live up to what the dead child was supposed to have been. The only way to correct that perception is to talk about the dead child as human and fallible just like everybody else.'

Tangible souvenirs of the dead brother or sister are also important for some siblings. Beryl Friend (Chapter 13) has cherished her sister's leather handbag for sixty years. Annie Richards (Chapter 7) liked having her sister's clothes to wear for a while. Barbara Talmage (Chapter 16) dearly wanted to be allowed to keep one of her brother's torches so that she could hug it to her in bed at night. Parents don't always recognize how important these little personal possessions might be to the surviving children. Either they throw everything away or they preserve the dead child's belongings as sacred relics.

'One way of coping with pain is to pretend that the child never existed and to scrub out every trace of them,' explained Betty Rathbone. 'The other extreme that people go to is to have the child's bedroom left as a shrine where nothing is ever allowed to be touched. The children mustn't play with this, that or the other, because it belonged to the dead child. Neither of these extremes is helpful.'

The ideal seems to be a question of balance, both in the family and in society as a whole. Society's attitudes towards death, particularly the death of children, and its treatment of the bereaved, have swung from the Victorians' sentimentality and didacticism to the next generation's taboos and secrecy. Neither stance is helpful or healthy. Robert Cecil in his work on changing attitudes in the nineteenth century makes this only too clear:

> To the charge that Victorians sentimentalised the death of their children has been added the allegation that they may have inflicted psychological damage by bringing them prematurely into contact with death. It is true, of course, that most Victorian parents regarded acquaintance with death as an integral part of the school of experience. . . . It must surely be apparent that, with death visiting almost every family with such regularity, any attempt to mask or evade the reality of death could not have succeeded, and would probably have made the situation worse. The problem facing Victorian parents was to reconcile themselves and their families to the harsh realities; this most of them achieved through their religious beliefs. . . .
>
> It is unhistorical to assume that children in the last century responded to death in the same way as children today; children's attitudes are largely conditioned by those of adults, and in our day the usual attitude is to evade the subject of death, to treat it as 'morbid' and, so far as possible, to exclude it from the home. Against such a background a child may well develop a troubled reaction, and one that seems to lack sympathy with adult bereavement. . . .
>
> Victorian parents have been condemned for clothing their children in black for months on end, and even putting babies in mourning. We can agree they carried these shows too far. On the other hand, we have been reminded by modern research, notably that of Lily Pincus,[2] that to pass over death in silence and offer no explanation of the disappearance of a well-loved member of the family can cause psychological damage that plagues a child when grown up.[3]

Betty Rathbone said she believed that society is currently moving towards a more balanced and healthy approach to its handling of the bereaved. Moving, but not yet quite there. 'I am hopeful, yes. I am hopeful that more people are free to go through the cycle of grieving and that at the end of it they accept that losses happen. We have to acknowledge that some losses are particularly untimely and an early sibling death comes into that context. There are traps, when dealing with bereaved children, but if you allow the child a fair amount of space, they're likely to give fair indications of what their needs are, but it is unlikely that it's right either to be wildly over-protective or to keep rubbing it in every five minutes.'

Finally, she pointed out that a person who, as a child, had suffered the loss of a sibling was not doomed to be damaged by the experience. 'I don't think it has to distort the whole of the rest of their development. It can never be the same, as though it hadn't happened, but that doesn't mean that the person has to be crippled. Assuming that children are helped to cope, then they are stronger than somebody who doesn't know how to cope. If they've learned how to communicate about being sad and so on, then they're not the people who are going to walk across the street when they see somebody coming who's just suffered a bereavement. They'll be able to go and give them a hug and say they're sorry to hear what's happened. They're likely to be more compassionate, more aware. Statistically, people who've had a significant loss when they're very young are more at risk of depression later in life than people who have not. But that still leaves lots of room for there to be success and resilience. It can be an opportunity for growth.'

NOTES

1. John Bowlby, *Attachment and Loss*. The Hogarth Press and the Institute of Psycho-Analysis, 1980.
2. Lily Pincus, *Death and the Family*. Faber, 1976.
3. Robert Cecil, *The Masks of Death*. The Book Guild, Ltd, 1991.

INDEX